D1726291

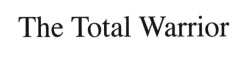

The Total Warrior

THE **TOTAL WARRIOR**

A 21ST CENTURY GUIDE TO MANHOOD, SPIRITUAL AWAKENING & THE WARRIOR WAY

STEWART BREEDING

LIBERTY HILL PUBLISHING

Liberty Hill Publishing
2301 Lucien Way #415
Maitland, FL 32751
407.339.4217
www.libertyhillpublishing.com

Due to the changing nature of the Internet, if there are any web
addresses, links, or URLs included in this manuscript, these may
have been altered and may no longer be accessible. The views
and opinions shared in this book belong solely to the author and
do not necessarily reflect those of the publisher. The publisher
therefore disclaims responsibility for the views or opinions
expressed within the work.

Unless otherwise indicated, Scripture quotations taken from the
King James Version (KJV)–*public domain.*

Paperback ISBN-13: 978-1-6628-4822-3
Ebook ISBN-13: 978-1-6628-4824-7

Dedicated to my brave brothers of Bravo Company,
1st Battalion 504th Parachute Infantry Regiment
82nd Airborne Division.
Strike Hold!

"Greater love has no one than this:
to lay down one's life for one's friends."
— John 15:13

Table of Contents

INTRODUCTION

This book has been a work in progress since the moment I took my first breath. It's the sole reason God spared my life so many times. Though I've included my story as background, this book is not about me. Instead, it is 100 percent about *you* and *your* awakening. I urge you to hear our Father's words as He speaks into your heart.

My hope in sharing with you a few of the epic moments in my life — moments that led to the writing of this book — is that you will remember the epic moments in your own life and learn how to grab hold of the truths you were taught and use them to transform your life and the world we live in. While our stories may be different, you and I are alike in the most basic, elemental ways.

I have fought through endless years of pain, deep scars, and demons who constantly scream words, such as *worthless*, *undeserving*, and *corrupt,* into my mind. While I still battle with sin and the addictions of my flesh every waking second, I also continue working to heal and inspire the endless line of souls who, sent by the Almighty, come to my doorstep every day. I am flawed, and so are you. There will only ever be one perfect Man, so empty yourself *right now* of all excuses, and read on.

The Total Warrior: A 21ˢᵗ century guide to Manhood, spiritual awakening & the Warrior Way is dedicated to my brothers in arms, the Ancient Saints, and our Warrior ancestors who paved the way. I am writing specifically for men, who have been under attack by Satan since the Garden of Eden. *The Total Warrior* is both a calling and a guidebook for all men aspiring to fill the chasm inside all our hearts and fill it with divine purpose.

In the pages that follow, my prayer is that you, too, will hear the voice of our Father as He speaks into your Warrior heart and awakens the sleeping giant inside each of us. I encourage you to empty yourself of all ideas concerning spirituality, mysticism, Christianity, and the infinite potential you have within your reach. Read each page earnestly and critically, challenging every word and sentence. Take nothing I say for granted so that, by the end, these ideas become your own.

My hope is that you will awaken to the divine truth found in the words and teachings of the greatest Warrior ever to live, the Lord and Savior, Jesus Christ. Take up your armor and prepare yourself for the greatest adventure of your life.

May God bless you on your journey.

Stewart Breeding

PART ONE

LIFE ON THE EDGE

CHAPTER ONE

Stairway to Heaven

I n the spring of 2002, I found myself staggering through the busy streets of Chicago, Illinois. I had spent the last ten years circling the drain. After leaving the Army, I fell prey to alcoholism, addiction, violence, and the constant distraction of my hormones.

I spent my few sober hours on a Zen cushion meditating or crashing parties at martial arts schools. If not, I banged weights at the dingiest, dankest gyms I could find. Only at these places could I find a sense of purpose, peace, stillness, and a momentary release from the war being waged over my soul.

Estranged from my family, I hadn't spoken to my parents or my son for almost six years. My son had been born in January, 1990, the day after I came home from Operation Just Cause in Panama. A few weeks earlier, two dear friends had been brutally killed in battle.

While in the service, I had stumbled onto a book, *"Harmony of Nature,"* by Mitsugi Saotome, a Master Aikido Instructor from Japan. A tremendous calling came over me, and I felt compelled to sacrifice everything and move to Sarasota, Florida, to study directly under Saotome. No one understood my motivations, especially since I would have to leave my infant son. I didn't understand either. But the vast brokenness of my mind, heart, and soul cried out for healing and the desire to dedicate my life for the sake of something I still do not completely comprehend.

Around 1994, after my tenure in Sarasota, I migrated to Nashville, Tennessee, for yet another epic period of drunken debauchery. Not long after, I traveled to Boulder, Colorado, again to study Aikido, this time under Hiroshi Ikeda, senior student to Saotome Sensei. While in Boulder, I hurled myself into rock climbing and mountain biking in a feverish, suicidal charge of near-death experiences. If not in the mountains, I trained two to three times a day, experimenting with random combinations of weight training, Jiu Jitsu, boxing, Aikido, and deeper levels of meditation.

I chose to work in bars by night and gyms by day. I could "legally" beat up drunkards and trade alcohol for cocaine and marijuana. Violence reigned in my life, and I was spinning out of control. I burned every bridge I could set ablaze. Finally, local law enforcement informed me I was no longer welcome in Boulder County. If something didn't change, I would be headed toward a violent death or a life of crime and eventual incarceration. A fresh start in a new town seemed to be my only option.

Suicidal, destitute, and without hope, I was at my darkest when I arrived in Chicago. As usual, it didn't take long to find a solid cocaine connection and a new favorite bar where I could inflict my pain on random, innocent bystanders just out for a night of fun with friends. Finally, after more than ten years of trying my darndest to kill myself, I got my chance.

I got myself into a knock-down, drag-out fight to the death in a rough-and-tumble bar in the wrong part of Chi-town.

Repeated kicks to my face and head shattered both jaws. My mouth hung almost to my chest, swinging like a piñata. My ribs were busted, my internal organs bruised and battered. I vaguely recall arriving at the emergency room where I fell into a three-day coma from massive head trauma.

When I awoke and peeled back the glue-like gunk that filled my eyes, I couldn't believe I was still alive. The reality of my broken body began to sink in, and I rubbed my jaws, which had been wired shut. Just then I noticed sunlight beaming through my window and shining directly on me. The rays, vivid and intensely white, highlighted every particle of floating dust. It was as though each beam encapsulated miniature galaxies, filled with stars, planets, and moons circling in a cosmic dance.

My heart and soul were filled by a presence. I knew I had been pulled from the jaws of death once again, saved for some unknown reason. Tears streamed down my face as I sat in pure and total surrender. In that moment, I had no doubt God had intervened on my behalf. There was simply no other reason for me to still be alive.

I couldn't comprehend why. I was a horrible person who had committed terrible acts of violence in and outside the military. A drunk, an addict, completely and utterly morally corrupt, I had turned my back and shaken my fist at God in favor of darkness and the counterfeit bliss of Zen Buddhism.

My body convulsed, and snot, tears, and blood poured down my face. From the deepest part of my heart, I cried out, "Why? I have nothing. I am nothing. What do You want me to do? If You want me to stay here, Lord, then You have to help me! I cannot do this alone."

I was released from the hospital with only 350 dollars to my name. My mouth remained wired shut for six weeks. With my body badly broken, I was unable to work, unable to pay for food or shelter. And I was living in what is, in my estimation, the most violent, unforgiving city in America.

By the sheer grace of God, several friends living in the area took me in, fed and clothed me, and gave me the time I needed to heal.

Divine providence was about to unfold.

While I was still living in Boulder, I had cultivated a relationship with a young student attending the University of Colorado. She now worked as a news anchor for a TV station in Coos Bay, Oregon. One day she called to check in and see how I was doing. By the end of the call, she had arranged airfare and traveling money, so I could go Oregon and get my life together.

I had long fantasized about living in the Pacific Northwest. Immediately upon landing in Coos Bay, I was flabbergasted by the power of the ocean and the immensity of the mountains that seemed to rise out of the water. Flowers, trees, and wildlife filled every vista. Wonder, coupled with a sense of comfort and protection, flooded my very soul. I was indeed where I was supposed to be.

I wasted no time in answering an advertisement in the local newspaper for a job as a front-desk attendant at Coos Bay Athletic Club. I was a seasoned lifter, as I had competed in powerlifting throughout my teen years. I had also made several failed attempts at becoming a personal trainer, a profession that barely existed in the nineties. I convinced the owners to let me attempt personal training services in exchange for a 70/30 split. They agreed, albeit reluctantly, making it a point to tell me that many before me had tried but failed. Despite the beauty of the city's surroundings, the economy of Coos Bay was one of the worst in Oregon, and few locals were financially able to pay for such a luxury.

I soon befriended a local physical therapist who had formed a local fibromyalgia group. I had never heard of fibromyalgia, and most of my training experience was with serious or professional athletes. The physical therapist encouraged me to observe her group and to meet over a dozen folks suffering with debilitating pain. Within weeks of attending her group, my schedule filled so quickly that I no longer had time to manage the front desk.

My confidence in my skillset grew in tandem with my client list. I found purpose and peace of mind, as I was finally working in the occupation for which I was destined. I watched in amazement as the people in my group overcame their debilitating pain. They didn't just get better; they were actually being healed from the afflictions of fibromyalgia and the dozens of other ailments that brought them into my world.

Word of my gifts and the odd miracles that seemed now to be commonplace spread like wildfire. Within a few months, I had a waiting list of potential clients. One of the clients, who quickly became integral to my success, was a psychologist who had a long-standing practice as a hypnotherapist. As we engaged in heated conversations about meditation, spirituality, and the powers of the mind, she encouraged me in a trade of services. I gladly obliged.

As much as I had fallen in love with Coos Bay, I knew it couldn't be a permanent home for me. I had been away from my son and family for over a decade, separated by more than 2000 miles. They didn't know if I was alive or dead. Guilt and concern for them grew to be unbearable.

I decided to risk everything and move back to Nashville to open my first business — a hybrid training center combining martial arts and strength training, along with living quarters to house both me and my best buddy, a traveling companion and fellow martial artist I had known for many years.

I was excited about restarting my life in Tennessee, yet I was terrified by the very thought of leaving the loving protection of the town God had hand-picked for me. Though I was now thirty-two, I still felt like a newborn calf whose legs were not quite yet beneath him. I lived on the precipice of relapse and trembled at the possibility of losing what I had gained.

What if I fell back into an existence occupied by alcoholism, addiction, and pain? The possibility of this nightmare becoming reality again motivated me to seek help from my hypnotist friend. During dozens of therapy sessions that precluded hypnotherapy, we spent long hours exploring my past, what had led me to Coos Bay, and who I had become while there.

Several weeks later, something happened in our very first hypnosis session. I rarely speak of this, but my life was changed forever. The therapist walked me through a type of guided meditation. As she directed me deeper and deeper into my psyche, I felt layers of muck and filth being lifted. While she continued speaking to me, another voice — not my own — spoke into my ear. Clear and unmistakable, this distinct voice sounded like a high-tech, surround-sound, Bose speaker, saying, "You are a holy man. You are a healer."

I had never used those words to describe anyone, especially myself. I had never spoken those words at all.

But there they were.

Trembling, I covered my face with my hands and wept uncontrollably. There was no mistaking from where this booming voice had come. The hypnotist held me, comforting me as I cried, totally shaken by what had transpired.

As I caught my breath, I asked her over and over if she had heard the voice or if she was playing some sort of cruel joke on me. I knew deep in my gut that something almost incomprehensible and truly divine had just taken place.

Fast Forward

Within a month of that profound experience, I left Coos Bay, never to return. I opened my dream studio shortly after arriving in Nashville. I am now in my eighteenth year as a gym owner and have become one of the most successful trainers and performance coaches in the country. I still pinch myself, as I recall the bizarre way God worked in my life and how many times He rescued me from the scythe of the Reaper.

I am a living example of—and testament to—the power of conviction, will, faith, redemption, and love.

Since that voice spoke into my heart so many years ago, I have helped heal hundreds of folks suffering from various orthopedic injuries, cancer, heart disease, diabetes, and mental and spiritual afflictions. On an even more personal level, I am blessed that the deep trauma I inflicted on my son and family has been mended. I reunited with my parents and sister after many wasted years.

Investing countless hours and tens of thousands of dollars, I worked with the finest instructors and operators in US Special Operations groups and Spetznaz, which consists of former Soviet Special Forces. I continually reflect on my experiences in combat and in some of the toughest schools in the military, including S.E.R.E (High Risk)—Survive, Evade, Resist,

Escape—one of the most brutal training procedures conducted by Special Operations.

By focusing misguided energy into the art and science of the tactical athlete, I learned to channel my aggression and deep-seated malevolence into a positive force. I am not vainly attempting to replace Matt Damon as the next Jason Bourne. My only desire is to give back to the country I love so much by helping push the performance envelope of our military, law enforcement, and civilian sentinels who warrant the same caliber of training.

I pray I can be of service in increasing their survivability, durability, and long-term physical and mental health. Moreover, I hope to unify all men charged to serve and protect His creation as Warriors for the Kingdom of God.

Mesmerized by the infinite potential of the human being and, having poured myself into the study of human performance, I have written three books on the subject.

I have traveled the world in search of answers and sat at the feet of the most gifted, enlightened spiritual masters alive today. I have been up, and I have been down. I have been there, done that. Nothing has escaped my feverish attempts to reach the pinnacle for a better view of the Grand Weaver who continues to navigate each second of my life. Though I continue to struggle every day for sobriety, I strive to live up to the words He spoke to me so many years ago.

Since that day, God has shared with me the inner workings of the universe and the hidden secrets uniting every religion, which call us to a life of mysticism, so that we may finally be in union with Him. I am awed by the transformations that turn suffering to blessings and the instant interactions of His presence as He tosses me around in the constant pinball game of life.

In 2020, after years of running both to and from the weight of knowing my destiny, I accepted Jesus Christ as my Lord and Savior.

Christianity is deeply rooted on both sides of my family and Appalachian ancestry. I had long been a theological student of Christianity and the ministry of Jesus. Knowing God's desire was for me to venture down a different path, my rebellious nature took me down many long and winding roads. But these detours had their purposes and finally led me into the waiting arms of His Son.

Though called to Christianity for quite some time, my ego just could not—or would not—take that last step. Then, out of the blue, my old platoon sergeant called and began talking about a four-day, intensive Christian program he had attended. The program, appropriately called the "Firebase," had been created and operated by former combat veterans who had come to Christ and started a mission group for veterans suffering with PTSD.

My sergeant's exact words were, "I don't know when they're going to do another one, but when they do, your ass is going!"

If you know anything about us vets, you know that the same sergeants who told you what to do, where to go, and how to be while you were in the service, still tells you what to do, where to go, and how to be as a civilian. And when he does, you damn well listen. Or at least I sure do, especially considering I pretty much worshipped the ground he walked on.

Within a few months, I attended a Firebase. Surrounded by my brothers-in-arms, I fell to my knees and gave my heart to Jesus.

I willingly surrendered my mind, body, heart, and soul to Christ and was touched yet again. With the majesty of the

Rocky Mountains at my side, a member of the mission prayed over me for hours. With my hands interlaced and buttressed against my forehead, I went completely deaf, and everything turned pitch black.

I began free-falling, tumbling helplessly into the abyss. My belly flip-flopped from the speed and G-forces tearing at me. Arms flailing, I scrambled for something to grab onto, as fear and absolute panic gripped my soul.

Suddenly, I pulled my arms back into my chest, sat straight up in my chair, and submitted to impending death. If these were my last moments, and my body was to be splattered all over Rocky Mountain High, then so be it. Minutes passed as sounds and the voices of my veteran brothers grew clearer. When I opened my eyes, it was as though I had never truly seen before. Everything was different, transformed. I quickly realized my eyes had not been transformed. I had.

Nothing has been the same since. Nothing else matters to me outside the immense duty I now feel to bring all those willing to listen, to encourage them to open their hearts to God and accept His Son Jesus Christ into their lives.

CHAPTER TWO

The Battle Between
Light and Darkness

*"We can easily forgive a child who is afraid of
the dark; the real tragedy of life is when men
are afraid of the light."*
—Plato

In 2013, researchers studying a small group of chimpanzees in southeastern Senegal stumbled upon a horrific site. A former alpha male they had nicknamed "Foudouku" had been brutally murdered and cannibalized. His body lay mutilated, prostrated in pools of his own dried blood. His limbs in tatters, his feet, toes, and fingers had been nearly bitten off. Members of his own tribe had stretched him out across the dry African landscape so they could beat him to death more easily.

Foudouku's ribs had been broken by repeated blows with rocks, fists, and feet. Even more appalling, several chimpanzees had bitten and ripped off chucks of flesh and then ingested them.

Until the works of Jane Goodall emerged in the 1970s, researchers, anthropologists, and scientists alike held to a long-standing belief that human beings were the only animal species on the planet with a propensity to kill its own kind. To be clear, I am speaking of homicide, cold-blooded murder, and tribal warfare—not the stalking and killing of another animal for primal reasons, such as hunger or survival.

Many studies over the last forty years have shown chimpanzees to be incredibly capable of the most heinous attacks. They not only assault their own kind, but their own families. This realization profoundly shook anthropologists. They had for centuries held tightly to the conviction that humankind alone is capable of the most demonic, sociopathic, and, yes, evil acts imaginable. It rocked them not because they had accidently stumbled upon the missing link, but because it spoke volumes about the truth of man's primal, malevolent nature and, quite possibly, their very own.

I am not an evolutionist. I do not believe we evolved from African apes, nor are we accidental space dust. There is nothing accidental about us or any of God's creation. We are the divine manifestation of God Almighty.

While this book is not an examination of the apologetics of Creation Theory vs. Evolution, it is important for us to understand that, even though our eternal souls are a divine product of God and are not subject to earthly laws, our physical bodies and our "*animal-ness*" is a shared product of all life on Earth and even the stars.

Our physical structure is composed of carbon from exploding stars and the very minerals in the Earth (Genesis 2:7). Life is generated by the "breath" of God, or what the ancient Brahmans of India call "Prana." This life energy is directly interjected into otherwise lifeless subatomic particles that create the physical structure we call matter, which, in turn, creates the cosmos we inhabit.

Everything in the universe is *interdependent* on some other thing for its existence. Our bodies are a mishmash of the entire universe, filled with the breath of God Himself. God's breath is the Holy Spirit, which contains the "mind" of God. We see the mind of God at work as the Master Director coordinating every subatomic particle in the universe into a cosmological dance of endless creation and transformation. The mind of God is the presence we all perceive, which binds the cosmos in unified purpose.

It is the force of nature that turns the food we eat into a human body. It instructs the birds how to fly in formation and head south for the winter. God's mind forces the wind to blow, the clouds to rain, the earth to spin, and the sun to shine. The mind of God permeates the entire universe of which all life and all forms are interconnected. These forms, or creation, are the body of God, which fulfills the Trinitarian Godhead of mind, body, and soul.

> *"And God said, let Us make man in Our image,*
> *after Our likeness" (Genesis 1:26).*

Only God is intra-dependent and *not* reliant on any other thing for His existence. As such, it is important for us to examine the shared characteristics of the inherited *"flesh"* and its accompanying addictions that manifest in our fallen state, like it does in other animals.

In Genesis, we learn the fallen state is the result of our ancestral parents, Adam and Eve, who single-handedly reduced humanity from its immortal, spirit-filled design living in Union with the Creator and His cosmos, into nothing more than an ape with a big brain. This is the product of Satanic corruption and choice—not evolution.

Since the end of World War II, countless books and empirical studies have attempted to shed light on Man's malevolent nature. One such study, "The Milgram Experiment," analyzed the willingness of its participants to obey the commands of an "authority figure." Participants, after being introduced, were assigned to be either teachers or learners. The teacher's job was to administer an electric shock to the learner, if the learner gave an incorrect answer to any of the teacher's questions. The shock administered by the teacher to the learner was labeled on what Professor Milgram affectionately termed the "Aggression Machine." The machine, measured with a series of switches moving from left to right, was clearly marked as follows.

- 15-60 Volts Slight Shock

- 75-120 Volts Moderate Shock

- 135-180 Volts Strong Shock

- 195-240 Volts Very Strong Shock

- 255-300 Volts Intense Shock

- 315-360 Volts Extreme Intensity Shock

- 775-420 Volts Danger Severe Shock

- 435-450 Volts XXX

As you can see, the level of shock administered by the teacher was identified, beginning with "slight shock" and, on its opposite end, "Danger, Severe Shock." Finally, in an obscure section at the far right of the machine is a 450v charge marked XXX. What the teacher did not know was that the learner was part of the experiment, and no shock at all would be administered once the teacher flipped the switch. The teacher was deceived into believing the administered shock was real and produced serious pain and possible injury.

Prior to the experiment, Dr. Milgram polled leading psychologists and sociologists. He asked them to hypothesize the percentage of study participants who would be willing to defy their own consciences and sense of morality, in order to administer a potentially lethal dose of electric shock to a fellow human being. The overwhelming majority of scientists polled agreed that less than 5 percent of study participants would be willing or capable of this level of malice. Milgram's conclusion following his experiment would be a source of contentious scientific controversy for years to come.

Of the 40 participants in the initial study, 65 percent were willing to administer a potentially lethal dose of electric shock to a fellow human being—a whopping 60% more than the 5 percent predicted. Two-thirds of the participants believed they had seriously injured or perhaps even killed someone they had met only hours before, simply because they were told to do so.

The Nature of Man

> **"A harmless man is not a good man. A good man is an extremely dangerous man, who has that under control."**
> **—Jordan B. Peterson**

What do Genesis, anthropological studies of chimpanzees, and psychological experiments on human obedience have to say about the nature of the animalistic flesh we all inhabit? What should we conclude about the potential darkness of humans, given massive historical evidence of our willingness to inflict heinous acts on our own kind through homicide, genocide, and warfare?

I am not referring to the sociopathic natures of men like Stalin, Hitler, Ivan the Terrible, or Mao. Nor am I considering those with psychopathic natures, like Manson, Gacy, Dahmer, or Bundy. I am talking about the true animal nature of typical men — men like you and me. What demons do you suppose lie under your bed at night? What monster lurks in your shadow? What horrors await you in the basement of your own psyche that you have never been willing to expose? Trust me, this darkness is in all of us.

This question of man's true nature is one of the oldest ever pondered and is the best place to start our journey. How can we arrive at our correct destination if we fail to comprehend the point of departure? When our ancestral parents sinned, they exchanged the interconnected grace of God for the addictions of the flesh and the physical world governed by the Prince of Darkness. Humanity has been the subject of a spiritual war ever since.

We are both the combatant and the prize of the war. If we are to begin fighting the good fight against the most ferocious enemy imaginable, the delusion that we are somehow accidental space dust or evolved apes must be thrown in the dumpster and burned to ashes.

Your goal for this book should be to peel back the onion (yes, you are the onion) to its most fundamental properties, and ask tough questions along the way. Therefore, the very first question we should ponder is, are we as human beings inherently good or inherently evil, and why?

What are the true obstacles we must overcome in order to live our best lives? What are the vehicles we can use to escape our earthly bonds? How deep is this rabbit hole, and are we willing to pay the price to get to the bottom?

In search of answers, we naturally look to horrors, such as Auschwitz, atrocities routinely found on the battlefield, or "ethnic cleansings," such as in Rwanda, Sudan, and the former Yugoslavia. We could also include the periodic discovery of dozens of bodies buried in yet another serial killer's backyard. We scratch our heads in disbelief, as we watch the evening news and wonder how these things happen. Who in their right mind could commit such cruelty? Sadly, we have to look no further than ourselves and man's perpetual fall from grace.

Man, left to his own devices, is inherently dark, capable of the most wicked acts imaginable. To add insult to injury, Man has a propensity to forget his own history and the immensely valuable lessons offered there. This leaves future generations vulnerable to their own destructive nature. This vulnerability, expedited by technological advancements in warfare, includes the propensity to embrace horrors on an unprecedented scale.

However, we are capable of subjugating this ferocity for the good of mankind. As opposed to our primate cousins, through Christ consciousness, we can learn to channel our primal nature, overcome egoic delusions, and use violence (or the threat of it) for the sake of peace and the protection of all sentient beings.

This subjugation requires massive amounts of discipline and a dedication to use one's God-given strength, skill, and power *only* in the promotion of peace, love, and self-defense. This precarious walk on the razor's edge is an intentional act of free will. It comes from the boldness and strength of those

who ae willing to walk the path of the Warrior, which I pray
you will now enter.

> *"Enter by the narrow gate; for wide is the gate*
> *and broad is the way that leads to destruction,*
> *and there are many who go in by it. Because*
> *narrow is the gate and difficult is the way*
> *which leads to life, and there are few who find*
> *it"* (Matthew 7:13-14).

The Human Dilemma

> *"Your task is not to seek for love, but merely*
> *to seek and find all the barriers within yourself*
> *that you have built against it."*
> *— Rumi*

Man is the only animal on the planet capable of *not* acting
on our primal, instinctive nature and the delusions of the flesh.
We control these impulses through the God-given gifts of free
will and conscience, intersected with the timeless, shared narrative of morality and ever-higher levels of spirituality. We are
human, yes. We are animal. But, at the same time, we are so
much more.

As previously stated, our bodies are literally the stars in
the heavens above and the totality of all life forms to have
ever existed. The whole of the universe is a living, breathing
organism of which you are apart. All of this is interdependent
on some previous thing, or things, for its very existence. You
were not born into this world. You were born out of it.

In summation, all things in existence now are endless combinations and variations of some previous thing, including our physical bodies. We are a mixture of the water we drink, the food we eat, the air we breathe, and the sun itself. Upon our demise, this process continues, as our bodies slowly transform and become the same fertile soil from which it came.

Nothing lost.

Nothing wasted.

Ashes to ashes, dust to dust.

Endless, cyclic transformation.

Our shared psychosis is that we are just this bio-body suit we inhabit with two eyes, two ears, two arms, two legs, and a creative brain, completely separate from every other organism and form in God's creation. The great awakening to Christ consciousness is the awareness of the dream curse placed on us before we were born and that all is one. Your true self is the entirety of the Logos Himself.

> *"Do you not know that your body is a temple of the Holy Spirit who is in you, whom you have received from God? You are not your own"*
> *(1 Corinthians 6:19).*

The human dilemma is that we are not just animal, not just human, not just stardust, we are *being*. We are aware of our own consciousness, or *beingness*, and also our physical animal-ness. We are the only species in the known universe capable of rising above our hormonal, primal instincts and expressing limitless potential for compassion, empathy, love, and spiritual growth.

We are also mindful of our own frailty and that of our brothers and sisters. As such, we are the only life form that realizes its own eventual demise. This awareness of death fuels man's quest for knowledge, purpose, and the answers to even more questions.

Genesis

> *"People use drugs, legal and illegal, because their lives are intolerably painful or dull. They hate their work and find no rest in their leisure. They are estranged from their families and their neighbors. It should tell us something that in healthy societies drug use is celebrative, convivial, and occasional, whereas among us it is lonely, shameful, and addictive. We need drugs, apparently, because we have lost each other."* —Wendell Berry

In Genesis, we are told that, in the beginning—on the sixth day—God made man, both male and female, in *"Our image,"* which means the divine fusion of mind, body, and soul. *"Then God saw everything that He had made, and indeed it was very good"* (Genesis 1:31 NKJV).

God gave man dominion over Earth. He gave him the Garden of Eden, food, water, purpose, love, and companionship. He also left Adam and Eve one clear restriction: *"Of every tree of the garden you may freely eat; but of the tree of the knowledge of good and evil you shall not eat, for in the day that you eat of it you shall surely die"* (Genesis 2:16-17 NKJV).

To God's great disappointment, this is exactly what Adam and Eve did. Their revolt caused Man's fall from grace, alongside the simultaneous ascent of Man's delusive ego, addiction

22

to the flesh, and the realization of his own frailty and inevitable death.

We all know this passage in the Old Testament. It's one of the oldest stories ever told. Its ancient origins began in oral tradition and were passed down through countless generations long before the advent of written language.

The classic accounts in the Old Testament, such as Adam and Eve, Cain and Abel, and Noah's ark, are filled with countless layers of wisdom, experience, and advice for how we are to live our best lives and return to our original godly existence. The historical debate of literal or metaphorical is minuscule compared to the treasure and impact these books impart on our daily lives and inner transformation. These ancient texts are filled with the shared reality of man's internal and external struggles. We wrestle with the enormity and complexity of a universe, which we are incapable of fully comprehending through our five senses and the demonic lie that we are somehow a cosmic accident.

Not only can Man not fully grasp the radical intricacies of a universe in which he is an integral part, but from his limited perspective it seems as though the universe is a violent, tumultuous place constantly attempting to destroy him. Immediately following the Fall of our ancestral parents, we see the rise of fear, separateness, and a perpetual sense of unfairness consume the heart of man.

In the story of Cain and Abel, we can see this dilemma unfold. Cain's hatred and jealousy for his brother consumes him, along with his distrust and anger with God for favoring Abel. In a blatant act of contempt for God, Cain murders his brother. Pure evil is spontaneously introduced into the world, infecting the children of Cain and the entirety of the human race in perpetuity.

Darkness Rises

> *"Light has nowhere to hide in the dark."*
> **—Matshona Dhliwayo**

Jordan Peterson, professor, psychologist, author turned theologian, has done a masterful job revitalizing these Old Testament stories. Through his writings and analysis, he connects them with the current psychological epidemic sweeping across the United States and its epic moral collapse. I find it absurdly ironic that a Canadian psychologist, not the clergy, has brought the powerful insight of the Holy Bible back into focus as the single greatest source of comprehending the complexity of humankind and our current death spiral.

Never in our nation's history have we seen such a rapid escalation in mental disease across all ages, races, and genders. Depression, addiction, anxiety, phobias, and suicides are more common than a cold, as are the medications prescribed to treat them. These disorders manifest into physical epidemics devouring the United States and Western cultures and include obesity, diabetes, heart disease, and cancer. All of these have been brought on by an expanding godless society and the systemic reaction to ever-increasing levels of internal and external stressors on our physical, mental, emotional, and spiritual well-being. At the same time, the rate of crimes, such as homicide, is exponentially increasing at a fevered pace.

In 2017, to the astonishment of the Church, Dr. Peterson successfully conducted a world-wide lecture tour, packed with standing-room-only audiences. He imparted a mixture of paternal wisdom blended with intuitive knowledge of Old Testament stories. These packed houses are mostly filled with young, impressionable men, struggling to navigate their way in a world filled with hate, greed, fear, and evil and void of worthy role models.

Over the last ten years, this void has exponentially grown and given rise to a new world order, or "Post-modern Collectivism." The slang term for this movement is "Cancel Culture," "Wokeness," or, to call it by its original name, Marxism. As the saying goes, "Those who forget history are doomed to repeat it" (George Santayana, American philosopher). Thus, the lessons learned from the ashes of countless millions murdered for the sake of a fictitious, godless, utopian society we refer to as "communism" loom upon us yet again.

CHAPTER THREE

A Time to Stand Up and Fight

Marxism and Cancel Culture are just a few of the unholy alliances we see manifested throughout the world today. Their central target includes all Western institutions. The shared belief at its core is that patriarchal (men) hierarchies who founded and developed the United States, Western cultures, capitalism, and the Church itself are systemically racist and the single source of all human suffering. As such, Post-modern Marxists believe the entirety of these patriarchal constructs must be destroyed at any cost, including the entirety of Judeo-Christian concepts.

Post-modern Marxism and unhinged leftist agendas, such as Critical Race Theory, have infested our corporations, schools, churches, universities, government, media, and even the military. To add insult to injury, mega-media corporations and big-tech social media companies are simultaneously merging with the federal government to force-feed the American people their shared Marxist narrative and to stifle all voices of discontent.

Facebook, Google, and Twitter have collaborated with massive tech giants like Apple and Samsung. Together, they manipulate artificial intelligence as a means of capturing the complete and total attention of its viewers, essentially transforming them from a consumer into a product.

Social media companies, through the use of AI, have created "avatars," or computer-simulated versions of ourselves, for each person who uses their platforms. In 2020, there were over 2.7 billion users on Facebook[1], translating to 2.7 billion different variations or avatars found on Facebook. Each variation has only one priority: To keep the user's attention and engagement at a maximum capacity and to disregard the nature of content it uses to accomplish its task.

In my opinion, this unprecedented experiment, which has largely taken place over the last ten years, is principally culpable for the exponential rise in the mental issues previously mentioned. It has, in addition, impacted the desocialization of our societies, especially among our youth. AI and high-capacity 5G cell phones are the epicenter of young people's lives (and many old enough to know better) in which they are the star of their own movie. The phone has become our friend, lover, parent, and teacher. No longer do we need to read and think critically or listen and communicate with precise language. No longer do we need companionship, love, affection, or understanding. We have our phones. The addiction to AI and the subsequent mental, physical, and social disease it produces could also, theoretically, produce an "Ending." An Ending is the very last of the species left inhabiting the Earth, prior to an extinction event.

According to a report recently published by Pew Research, 25 percent of millennials will likely never be married.[2]

---

[1]   https://acodez.in/facebook-users-worldwide/

[2]   https://relevantradio.com/2021/10/millennials-and-marriage/

According to the U.S. Census Bureau's Current Population Survey, in 2014, 47.6 percent of women between age 15 and 44 had never had children, up from 46.5 percent in 2012.[3] The census data is backed up by data from the National Center for Health Statistics, which showed in a recent report there were just 62.9 births for every 1,000 women ages 15-44 in 2013, an all-time low.[4]

Is social media to blame? Impossible to know, but we can clearly see attacks on Judeo-Christian concepts, such as marriage between a man and woman and the incredible joy and responsibility of child rearing, infest our society via social and television media. To add insult to injury, online dating sites make it incredibly simple and vogue for young, single people to browse countless photos and bios of their ideal candidate and engage in sexual relations without ever even meeting face to face. Who needs the downer of marriage and kids?

A 2013 study published in the Journal of Sexual Medicine suggests that Erectile Dysfunction (ED) is more common among younger men than previously thought.[5] Researchers found that ED affected 26 percent of adult men under 40. Almost half of these young men had severe ED, while only 40 percent of older men with ED had severe ED. There are more alarming statistics than that, though, like a July 2020 survey of 5,800 men in which 23 percent of respondents under 35 reported erectile dysfunction. What is to blame? Quite possibly, widespread

---

[3] www.armstrongeconomics.com/world-news/civil-unrest/
    are-we-getting-dumber/

[4] https://www.cdc.gov/nchs/data/nvsr/nvsr63/nvsr63_02.pdf

[5] https://medicalxpress.com/news/2013-06-patients-newly-diagnosed-
    erectile-dysfunction-young.html

addiction to pornography has caused unprecedented rates of erectile dysfunction in young men.

On average, most young people watch porn for the first time by the age of 13. For most boys and an increasing number of girls, it is the beginning of a lifelong habit. Around 80 percent of men and 30 percent of women (45 percent if you include only women who watch with their partners) view porn weekly. The internet and advances in technology are largely to blame. PornHub says 76 percent of its traffic comes from mobile phones[6] —and more people than ever are watching due to COVID-19 keeping people at home. And here are more startling statistics:

- 28,258 users are watching pornography every second

- $3075.64 is spent on porn every second on the internet, primarily via cell phones

- 88 percent of scenes in porn films contain acts of physical aggression, and 49 percent contain verbal aggression

- 1 in 5 mobile searches are for pornography

- 90 percent of teens and 96 percent of young adults accept porn as normal

- Teens and young adults 13-24 believe that not recycling is morally worse than viewing pornography[7]

---

[6] https://www.cnet.com/news/features/
porn-addiction-is-ruining-lives-but-scientists-arent-convinced-its-real/

[7] https://www.ncregister.com/blog/
what-every-parent-needs-to-know-about-pornography

- Only 43 percent of teens believe porn is bad for society

- 43 percent of senior pastors and youth pastors say they have struggled with pornography in the past, while only 7 percent offer a ministry program for those struggling with addiction

- 68 percent of divorce cases involve one party meeting a new lover over the internet[8]

- 56 percent of divorces involve one party having an "obsessive" interest in pornographic websites

- 70 percent of wives of sex addicts could be diagnosed with PTSD

If that were not insane enough, let us examine the transgender issue for a moment. Clearly, we can see a colossal shift in awareness generated around the LGBTQ community with special attention being paid to the transgender population. In Canada, Europe, and parts of the United States, there is a massive effort to write into law the specific use of transgender pronouns. The LGBTQ community, in cahoots with the progressive left, have conducted an all-out assault on young, impressionable minds around the western world to rewrite and destroy Judeo/Christian concepts and biological, scientific truths. Social media and the internet are their battlefield of choice.

Alongside potential unconstitutional laws enforcing "correct pronoun usage," the transgender movement insists gender is a social construct, not a biological certainty. They believe that

---

8 file:///C:/Users/Evelyn/Downloads/Pornography-Statistics.pdf

it is completely up to the individual to decide what gender they are and, that at any given moment, they are free to change their minds. As of today, some schools and teachers will address the transgender person not only by their gender of choice but by a different name altogether, unbeknownst to the parents.

Doctors and psychologists in many parts of the world must now diagnose their young clients with severe Gender Dysmorphia any gender confusion exists, no matter if their scientific conclusion proves different, such as the client is just possibly gay. A massive battle is underway to allow young teenagers the right, "without parental consent," to inject sex hormones, such as testosterone, into their bodies, altering the natural development of puberty permanently, or possibly even allowing them to obtain sex-change surgery.

In the UK, young people referred for "gender treatment" has increased from 97 in 2009 to 2,510 in 2017-2018, a more-than 4,000 percent increase in 10 years.[9] This procedure forever changes the natural, God-given gender of the child when a large percentage are just simply confused about their sexuality (possible homosexual or bisexual).

But wait, there is more!

In the winter of 2020, the worst pandemic (COVID-19) since the outbreak of Spanish Influenza in 1918 swept around the world. Fear, distrust, and mass hysteria spread as quickly as the virus itself. Massive lockdowns of entire cities and states ensued, along with tyrannical assaults on the freedoms and civil liberties of every citizen. Some fifteen months later, we are just

---

[9] https://www.christianpost.com/news/uk-investigating-why-gender-dysphoria-children-increased-over-4000-percent-10-years.html

beginning to discover the depth of lies and deceit that surround COVID-19. These include:

- The origin—which overwhelmingly points to an unintentional or intentional release from the Wuhan Institute of Virology in China. More evidence points to the fact that Dr. Anthony Fauci, (Director of the National Institute of Health and lead point man for the United States in combating the COVID pandemic), not only knew within the first week that the virus was manmade but that his organization very likely directly funded the Gain of Function research, which created the virus.

- At least half of the United States is either reluctant or unwilling to vaccinate with the experimental MRNA vaccines, which during 2020 were still only in emergency- use authorization (non-FDA approved). There are two important reasons for this skepticism about the vaccines: First, people are worried because doctors are voicing their concerns regarding the MRNA vaccines. In addition, individuals who have had illness-related symptoms from these vaccines are speaking out. (Some people have died) Second, natural immunity from having survived the virus, seems to be much greater than the immunity the vaccine provides, but is, ironically not recognized by government or medical authorities.

- There continues to be massive data supporting therapeutics, such as Hydroxychloroquine and Ivermectin, yet their use is being shadow-banned or completely removed from social media, (via the censorship campaign forged between social media giants and Federal Government).

- The CDC is still pushing the use of masks on the "non-vaccinated," even for children as young as two years old. They are suggesting the use of experimental MRNA vaccinations for those as young as five years old. They continue to push this narrative even though no meta-analysis proves the efficacy of mask usage to prevent a viral, airborne transmission. Dr. Fauci himself has stated in emails, "Masks are really for infected people to prevent them from spreading infection to people who are not infected rather than protecting uninfected people from acquiring infection. The typical mask you buy in the drug store is not really effective in keeping out virus, which is small enough to pass through material. It might, however, provide some slight benefit in keeping out gross droplets if someone coughs or sneezes on you." He added, "I do not recommend that you wear a mask, particularly when you are going to a very low risk location." [10]

- Vaccine passports continue to increase in frequency amongst large corporations, concerts, sport venues, and especially travel. These "passports," showing that the bearer has been vaccinated against COVID, must be used to gain access to specific areas.

More insanity is being loaded onto the backs of free citizens around the world on a daily basis. I shudder to think at what

---

[10] https://stream.org/faucis-mask-flip-flop-explained-by-economics/

will unfold as we dig deeper into what seems to be the only man-made, bioengineered pandemic in human history. God willing, it will be the last.

Violent riots, looting, and the physical burning of cities powered by the violent threats of Marxist organizations, such as Black Lives Matter and Antifa (anti-fascist), continue to spread throughout America. Calls to defund the police by the Democratic Party and the demonization of law enforcement have become a call to arms among leftist radicals. In their view, our racist society is to blame for all criminal behavior, rather than the perpetrator, especially if that perpetrator is a person of color. As such, crime and homicide are at epidemic proportions.

According to a report from the NCCCJ (National Commission on COVID-19 and Criminal Justice) homicides increased by 36 percent across 28 major U.S. cities—including Los Angeles, Atlanta, Detroit, and Philadelphia—between June and October 2020, when compared to the same time period the previous year.[11] Per the GVA, (Gun Violence Archive) 2020's total gun homicides had, by the end of October, already exceeded that of the past four years.[12]

The Presidential general election of 2020 between Republican incumbent Donald Trump and the Democratic nominee Joe Biden was demonstrably manipulated by social

---

[11] j https://news.yahoo.com/2020-end-one-americas-most-142333492.html

[12] https://www.gunviolencearchive.org/

and television news media conglomerates, who controlled and censored any information contrary to their objectives.

Five swing states (Michigan, Georgia, Arizona, Pennsylvania, Wisconsin) unconstitutionally changed election laws moments before the general election, allowing for unsolicited, unverified mail-in ballots, completely circumventing the electoral process outlined in each state's Constitution.[13] These unprecedented actions were perceived by many as an all-out assault on our Republic and heaped even more hatred, distrust, and contempt into the fray.

Multiple court cases were filed across the United States including a joint lawsuit of twenty-one states, concerning the unconstitutionality of the 2020 General Election. No court, to include the most powerful, righteous court in the land (United States Supreme Court) was willing to hear any arguments or to review any evidence of fraud. All cases brought to the courts were either not allowed to be introduced or dismissed on technicalities.

Finally fourteen months after the election, on January 28th, 2022 a Pennsylvania court struck down Act 77, the law that established no-excuse mail voting in Pennsylvania, saying it violated the state constitution.

As a result of the failures of the courts and the onslaught of attacks on America's civil liberties by Federal and State governments, the powder keg, which had been building for more than a year, finally blew.

On January 6[th,] a small group of embattled, frustrated conservative citizens raided the doors of the U.S. Capitol in

---

[13] https://www.texasattorneygeneral.gov/news/releases/ag-paxton-sues-battleground-states-unconstitutional-changes-2020-election-laws

violent protest. During the protest, Ashli Babbitt, a 35-year-old, unarmed Air Force veteran was shot in the neck and killed by Capitol police. Not only is it taboo and social suicide to inquire about the motivations of the protestors in the Capitol riot, but to this day no investigation has taken place into the death of Ashli Babbitt.

As of the writing of this book, over a year has passed and America's cities are still under siege. The southern border with Mexico has been completely abandoned, and over two million illegal aliens have migrated into the United States. We are beginning to see reports that the Biden Administration and the United States Air Force are transporting these illegal aliens across the United States in what seems to be an overt attempt to manipulate the electoral system.

The CDC has unconstitutionally subverted the 4th Amendment and suspended our rights to private property, declaring it unlawful to evict a delinquent tenant.[14] The Biden administration withdrew all forces from Afghanistan leaving countless Americans behind and squandering the lives of 2,313 American soldiers killed in action. Within two weeks the Taliban has once again taken over this godforsaken land and placed a bullseye on every American citizen.

The 45th President Donald Trump has been vanquished from social media platforms and his supporters demonized. Censorship and the loss of 1st Amendment rights seem routine. Calls to repeal the 2nd Amendment and "the right of the people to keep and bear arms" are heralded by none other than the very Chief Executive who swore an oath to protect the Constitutional Rights of his constituency, not repeal them.

---

[14] https://reason.com/2021/10/03/how-the-cdc-became-americas-landlord/

Our Constitution and even the three equal branches of government are under an all-out assault by progressive socialists and Marxists in a blatant attempt to rewrite history and destroy the greatest experiment of a free people ever to exist. This degradation of our culture, country, and society created by leftist anarchists is also simultaneously happening in every other Western or capitalist nation around the world, including Europe.

Australia's military has been deployed to enforce an eighteen-month long lockdown of its citizens with no end in sight. Hundreds of thousands all over Europe actively protest the EU's sanctioning of a COVID Passport to prove vaccination. France has declared it unlawful to enter public spaces without proof of vaccination. Those caught without "their papers" are sentenced to no less than six months in prison. Business owners who do not enforce these "laws" are condemned to a year behind bars.

France's military leadership has warned its government multiple times concerning an impending civil war. Their concerns are brought on by an increase of Islamism, crime, and incredibly bizarre, leftist policies, which have decimated the culture and moral character of France. Over the last several years, well over a thousand Christian churches have been burned or vandalized, including Notre Dame. The government and Church refuse any attempt to label these acts as hate crimes and flatly refuse any effort to lay blame at the feet of leftist extremist or the Islamic fundamentalists they protect.

While this madness unfolds, the hypocrisy of the "Woke Church" seems to know no bounds. The sanctity of life and the loving protection of the innocent, poor, and ill are the very foundations of Christian tradition and the teachings of Jesus Christ. The clergy continues to avoid taking a stance to protect the innocent and turns a blind eye to self-proclaimed Christian politicians and members of their own congregations who continue to advocate for federally funded abortions. During the lockdown of 2020, Planned Parenthood alone aided in the slaughter of 354,871 innocent, unborn children, paid for by American tax dollars.[15] The total number is estimated at 903,000.[16] While abortion clinics remained open for business, the church itself was told to close its doors, and gladly obliged.

Privately held businesses, corporations, and non-profit organizations dwell in a state of fear, compliance, and complacency setting the scene for a new form of fascism led by the largest financial institution in the world: BlackRock.

> *"Pay no attention to the man behind the curtain.*
> **—Wizard of Oz**

According to Wikipedia, BlackRock, Inc. is an American multinational investment management corporation based in New York City.[17] Founded in 1988, initially as a risk management and fixed-income institutional asset manager, BlackRock is the world's largest asset manager, with $9.5 trillion in assets under management as of October 2021.

That equals almost half of the United States annual GDP.

To give you a small example of how deep and dark this rabbit hole goes, Wikipedia is owned by a nonprofit organization, Wikimedia. Wikimedia's largest contributor is Google. Google's largest shareholder is the Vanguard Group, Inc., the

---

[15] https://www.cnsnews.com/article/national/michael-w-chapman/
planned-parenthood-performed-354871-abortions-fiscal-2020

[16] https://www.abort73.com/abortion_facts/us_abortion_statistics/

[17] https://en.wikipedia.org/wiki/BlackRock

second largest financial institution in the world. Vanguard is the largest shareholder in BlackRock, and BlackRock is the largest shareholder in Vanguard.

BlackRock owns practically every major brand conceivable. Its board members consist of leaders from the largest corporations in the world to include social and news media empires, Big Tech, Big Food, Big Pharma, Big Energy, Big Airlines, Big Medical, Big Insurance, Big Banks, Big Freight/Trucking/Shipping, Big Agriculture, Real Estate, Military Defense Contractors, etc.

Basically, if you can think of a name brand, BlackRock owns a large chunk of it. One company literally dominates the economic landscape of the free world.

BlackRock is the financial arm of a multi-pronged, fascist beast, which I believe is hell-bent on a totalitarian takeover of the world. I don't say this lightly or without merit. This statement is based on the anti-democratic, inhumane policies and actions of BlackRock's companies, such as the censorship of conservative citizens. They squash any dissenting voices, especially those that might question the legitimacy of the 2020 general election or object to the coordinated narrative surrounding COVID-19.

Media outlets such as Facebook, Google, YouTube, Twitter, CNN, NBC, ABC, CBS, The New York Times, The Washington Post, just to name a few, speak with a unified "progressive voice," because they are owned and operated by BlackRock That voice was responsible for four straight years of "Fake News," lies, and fear campaigns intended to destroy President Donald Trump and his MAGA (Make America Great Again) movement at any cost. It is also the same voice demanding that everyone get in lockstep to take an experimental vaccine that does not stop infection or the spread of the disease and begins to lose its efficacy within months.

This massive media blitzkrieg unfolds while proven therapeutics, such as ivermectin, hydroxychloroquine, and monoclonal antibodies, are either federalized, making them almost impossible to find or completely banned from use by physicians. According to many researchers, an estimated 500,000 Americans have unnecessarily died due to government policies and the denial of therapeutics.

Dr. Anthony Fauci, the Director of NIH, was responsible for the funding of gain-of-function research of Corona viruses in the Wuhan Institute of Virology, Wuhan, China, the epicenter of the COVID-19 pandemic.

Dr. Fauci has spearheaded an unprecedented movement, again led by the fusion of government and "fake news" conglomerates, to remove from hospitals and their physicians any and all therapeutics pertaining to COVID-19 treatment, except one: remdesivir.

Remdesivir is owned by Gilead Sciences Inc. and is the ONLY so-called therapeutic offered in hospitals in the United States and abroad to treat advanced disease brought about by COVID-19. My father and my son were hospitalized with COVID. Both were denied any alternative treatment, except for remdesivir. My father, a veteran of the Korean Conflict, died three days after entering the hospital.

Gilead's largest stockholders are, not surprisingly, BlackRock and Vanguard.

This excerpt from an article taken from Science.org pertains to the enigma of Remdesivir.

"October was a good month for Gilead Sciences, the giant manufacturer of antivirals headquartered in Foster City, California. On 8 October, the company inked an agreement to supply the European Union with its drug remdesivir as a treatment for COVID-19—a deal potentially worth more than $1 billion. Two weeks later, on 22 October, the U.S. Food and Drug Administration (FDA) approved remdesivir for use against the pandemic coronavirus SARS-CoV-2 in the United States—the first drug to receive that status. The EU and U.S. decisions pave the way for Gilead's drug into two major markets, both with soaring COVID-19 cases.

"But both decisions baffled scientists who have closely watched the clinical trials of remdesivir unfold over the past 6 months—and who have many questions about remdesivir's worth. At best, one large, well-designed study found remdesivir modestly reduced the time to recover from COVID-19 in hospitalized patients with severe illness. A few smaller studies found no impact of treatment on the disease whatsoever. Then, on 15 October—in this month's decidedly unfavorable news for Gilead—the fourth and largest controlled study delivered what some believed was a coup de gras: The World Health Organization's (WHO's) Solidarity trial showed that remdesivir does not reduce mortality or the time COVID-19 patients take to recover.

"Science has learned that both FDA's decision and the EU deal came about under unusual circumstances that gave the company important advantages. FDA never consulted a group of outside experts that it has at the ready to weigh in on complicated antiviral drug issues. That group, the Antimicrobial Drugs Advisory Committee (AMDAC), mixes infectious disease clinicians with biostatisticians, pharmacists, and a consumer

representative to review all available data on experimental treatments and make recommendations to FDA about drug approvals—yet it has not convened once during the pandemic.

"The European Union, meanwhile, decided to settle on the remdesivir pricing exactly 1 week before the disappointing Solidarity trial results came out. It was unaware of those results, although Gilead, having donated remdesivir to the trial, was informed of the data on 23 September and knew the trial was a bust."[18]

As of January 2021, two years into the pandemic, remdesivir continues to be the only therapeutic offered in hospitals in the United States, even though doctors, nurses, hospitals, and government officials know its efficacy is, at minimum, questionable.

The censorship of critical information pertaining to our health is extreme and egregious and could quite possibly spark yet another civil war. Social media companies "shadow ban" or completely remove any voice of dissent, such as Senator Rand Paul and Congresswoman Marjorie Taylor Greene, a bold voice of the MAGA movement, and Dr. Robert Malone, the creator of the MRNA technology. Dr. Malone is one of many thousands of leading doctors, researchers, and scientists sounding alarm bells concerning:

- o Illegal, unethical, inhumane denial of therapeutics to treat COVID patients in hospitals

- o Massive government payouts to hospitals for treating COVID-positive patients to include incentives for

---

[18] https://citizenwells.substack.com/p/remdesivir-fact-vs-fiction-part-5

treatment of advanced disease (ventilators) and even death

o Denial of informed consent pertaining to the health risks and injuries associated with MRNA vaccine

o Massive levels of unnecessary, unproven vaccination (3-4 booster injections) to millions across the globe

o Vaccination of healthy children with little to no risk from COVID-19

If you think the dubious actions of fake news and fascist social media empires is concerning, pull back the curtain a little more and look at BlackRock's political affiliations.

The three major political organizations connected to BlackRock are the Council on Foreign Relations (headquartered in New York City USA), The Council on Foreign Relations (headquartered in Berlin), and the World Economic Forum (headquartered in Davos, Switzerland). Strangely enough, Larry Fink, CEO of BlackRock, sits on both the boards of the Council on Foreign Relations and the World Economic Forum.

The Council on Foreign Relations is a powerful, leftist think tank largely responsible for policy/narrative creation of the Democratic Party and the current administration occupying the White House. The Council is strategically interconnected with the European Council on Foreign Relations, which is a leftist, pan-European think tank. Both think tanks have their roots in pro-socialist democracy movements heralded by advocates such as Woodrow Wilson and Count Richard von Coudenhove-Kalergi.

I believe the World Economic Forum to be the epicenter for the concept of a one-world government and the source behind the shared insanity and mass-formation psychosis infecting every country around the world concerning COVID-19 and their coup de gras, "greatest emergency of our time," the Global Warming [and Endangered Species] Initiative.

The World Economic Forum is also interconnected with three major non-profits with shady reputations and affiliations to hardcore Marxist organizations, like ANTIFA and Black Lives Matter. The Open Society Foundations, led by none other than George Soros, The Gates Foundation, led by Bill and Melinda Gates, and the Clinton Foundation, led by Bill and Hillary Clinton, are primarily responsible for holding the entire nation hostage during 2019 and 2020.

The COVID pandemic has conveniently made BlackRock the undisputed largest, wealthiest, most powerful monopoly in the history of the world. They control the news and its narrative. They control the politicians and bureaucrats of every democratic nation on Earth (G7) to include the United Nations. They control the CEOs and leadership of every major business globally. They are Wall Street. They are the FED. They are the undisputed wizard behind the curtain, pulling and tugging at the strings of eight billion puppets inhabiting the planet who dwell in the matrix they have designed.

Every democratic nation on Earth is attempting to force their citizens, no matter their individual medical histories, to take an experimental vaccine or lose their freedom. These citizens must also show proof (universal vaccine cards) of their submission to authoritarianism in order to travel, work, and play. This is unquestionably a throwback to the Jewish Holocaust and the forceful exhibition by the Nazi Party for millions of Jews to wear the Star of David on their sleeves, so they would be more easily targeted for slaughter.

Those who have been watching closely since 2016 know that something is amiss. I have struggled over the last several years to connect the dots, so I can put some kind of method to this madness we see unfolding every day. Please, form your own opinions, don't take me at my word. Do your own research, as I have done, and base your opinions—not on the shared narrative being shoved down our throats—but on solid, truthful information and what we all clearly see unfurling before our eyes. Begin by asking these questions:

o   Who owns the companies who are manufacturing the experimental MRNA vaccines?

o   Who owns the hospitals making billions from the pandemic?

o   Who owns the corporate giants pushing for unconstitutional mandates of vaccines and the new "woke" agenda?

o   Who owns the social media and news companies charged with "fact-checking" of any mis- or disinformation pertaining to the vaccine and pushing the fear-mongering propaganda of COVID?

o   Who funds the political organizations and campaigns of government officials around the world who are perpetrating these crimes against humanity and freedom?

o   Which political party gained the most from the Covid-19 Pandemic?

Does anyone see a conflict of interest here? Are you beginning to get my point?

If BlackRock is not the Anti-Christ, they will do until the true Anti-Christ is on the scene. Once again, from my vantage point, BlackRock is the single greatest threat to freedom the world has ever known. Only God knows why they continue to forcefully push jab after jab of unproven, untested vaccine into billions of people every day for a disease that has a 99% survival rate (and increasing every day).

What are we going to do about it? Where are the leaders willing to stand against this fascist beast and destroy it before it destroys us? This will undoubtedly have to be a collaborative effort of federal and state governments, the Church, citizen outreach, and privately owned businesses, but it starts with us and our willingness to stand up and speak out. Undeniably, this requires massive levels of courage and the willingness to take some serious hits both socially and professionally. Even so, we must speak out or share the same fate as the citizens of Auschwitz who sat and watched as 1.3 million people were turned into a pile of ash.

Never in history has society so desperately needed new Davids to stand up and face the Goliaths currently destroying our freedoms and way of life. Never have we needed a small group of brave Warriors to stand against totalitarianism as did King Leonidas and his mighty 300 in the battle of Thermopylae. Never has Lady Liberty been so desperate for a new generation of Warrior heroes to step out of the mighty shadows of their ancestors and write their own stories. Never have we so needed brave men to step up and protect the God-given gifts of life, liberty, and the pursuit of happiness.

Answering the Call

"History will be kind to me for I intend to write it."
— Winston Churchill

Almost every story in the Bible has at its core the antagonist, life itself, accompanied by the seemingly opposite bookends we refer to as good and evil. As its protagonist, we see the rise of the hero archetype, who must first battle his own fears and inner demons before stepping onto any battlefield. This is especially true of the battlefield we are faced with today.

Crime, murder, and riots in the streets are on the rise. Moral decay, social collapse, and even civil war seem to be real possibilities, not just in the United States but in all free Western societies. If we know our Bible, it is easy to believe all this madness is interconnected. Most assuredly, we are living the end times or at least heading in that direction. The signs are too many and darkness too pervasive. This is not the first time society has faced such monstrous dilemmas, but without courageous, brave men willing to sacrifice personal and professional security, it quite possibly could be the last.

This book is a calling and a step-by-step manual for all men willing to listen, to answer the call of your Warrior hearts, to awaken, and get in the fight.

We were born into a war. Not one with bullets and bombs, but rather, a war for our hearts and souls, a spiritual war that began long before man came to existence and is playing out before our very eyes.

Everyone is a combatant in this war, whether we like it or not. The stories of heroes in the Old Testament are designed to deliver wisdom and life skills that came from countless conquests, triumphs, and failures of our ancestors. Every story, no matter the cast and characters, no matter how seemingly different, always has the same plot. Life is a big, angry giant trying to stomp on our heads—and all we have are slingshots.

It is as though a massive flood is intent on wiping out all life on the planet, but you have built a hell of a boat (even though everyone thinks you're crazy). Picture an evil king or pharaoh drunk on power and hell-bent on destruction, and you must lead your people to safety and freedom. In all of these stories, men are encouraged by the Almighty to rise, come to terms with their inner demons, and face the enemy with chins up, shoulders back, placing one foot in front of the other.

The entirety of the animal kingdom and the fallen state of humanity often take the low road in this fight and default to immorality, cruelty, gang mentality, and cowardice. This low road is evidenced by the murder and mutilation of our chimpanzee friend Foudouku, the atrocities of Auschwitz, and the rioting and looting of America in 2019-20.

In stark contrast, our hero stands alone in the world with all odds against him. He must dig deep into his Warrior heart, face adversity head on, and, through his free will granted to him by God Almighty, accept the consequence or glory of his actions.

From a purely psychological perspective, studies clearly show that facing our fears head on is not only psychologically healthier but also physiologically and spiritually beneficial. The biblical stories previously mentioned serve to graciously impart on us what science is just now beginning to understand, that running *to* our fear is far better than running away.

Rising up and facing both internal and external demons is the wisest, healthiest course of action. We have an immense responsibility to live up to the potential God Almighty placed upon humankind 2000 years ago, as clearly demonstrated by the living example given to us by His Son, Jesus Christ.

My prayer is that this book will offer its readers inspiration, motivation, and a realistic framework for how we, as men, can develop our Warrior spirit, heart, mind, and body, in addition to the skillsets to free us from the shackles of original sin, raising us up to our infinite potential, as gifted by our Maker.

My hope is that the pages that follow will outline the interconnected, historical traditions of Warriors and sages across space and time. Its content will simultaneously offer readers an "instruction manual," guiding each of us up the stairway to heaven, and into the waiting arms of our loving, Heavenly Father. I pray my words will build depth, wisdom, strength of character, body, and spirit, as well as the ability to persevere in the face of chaos and evil at our doorstep.

A series of questions are included at the end of the book. These questions are designed to awaken Christ consciousness and nudge you into deep levels of contemplation. Take your time answering, leaving nothing to the imagination. I recommend reading the entire book then go back and review the text and answer the questions. Our Heavenly Father and His Son know you better than you know yourself. Hiding truths will only delay your growth. Share the deepest, darkest parts of yourself, and replace that darkness once and for all with the light of God's kingdom.

Nietzsche said, "You can judge one's character by the amount of truth they can handle." Sadly, we will never realize our ultimate potential while here on Earth. There will only ever be one perfect Man who so graciously embodied the Warrior spirit. We can only look deeply inside ourselves and discover the truth about who we are and who we are not, no matter how ugly or terrifying it may be.

Only the Warrior is willing and able to handle the endless knocks of life and still persevere. Only a Warrior can fight the greatest battle ever fought, the one for his very soul and the future of humanity.

CHAPTER FOUR

THE WAY of the WARRIOR

"So live your life that the fear of death can never enter your heart. Trouble no one about their religion; respect others in their view, and demand that they respect yours. Love your life, perfect your life, beautify all things in your life. Seek to make your life long and its purpose in the service of your people. Prepare a noble death song for the day when you go over the great divide.

"Always give a word or a sign of salute when meeting or passing a friend, even a stranger, when in a lonely place. Show respect to all people and grovel to none. When you arise in the morning give thanks for the food and for the joy of living. If you see no reason for giving thanks, the fault lies only in yourself. Abuse no one and no thing, for abuse turns the wise ones to fools and robs the spirit of its vision. When it comes your time to die, be not

like those whose hearts are filled with the fear
of death, so that when their time comes, they
weep and pray for a little more time to live their
lives over again in a different way. Sing your
death song and die like a hero going home."
—*Tecumseh, Shawnee Warrior Chief*

There is no shortage of infamous Warriors, nor is there a lack of yarns told about the epic lives they lived. When one reads the above quote from Chief Tecumseh, it is obvious that his beliefs, worldview, and actions are all shared values reflected in every religion and Warrior tradition. You could remove Tecumseh's name and replace it with Bodhisattva, Nelson Mandela, Mahatma Gandhi, or Martin Luther King. This value system Tecumseh speaks of penetrates time and space and is undoubtedly divine in nature. Therefore, it is accessible to all souls seeking a deeper knowledge of self and the universe we share.

The Warrior tradition is as old as humankind. It is the essence of manhood, imprinted directly into our molecular code (DNA) by our Heavenly Father Himself. Every man born into this earthly realm is, above all else, a Warrior at his core. The gaping hole we all feel in our lives can only be filled with our true purpose: to single-mindedly protect and serve God's Creation.

The Warrior tradition, its shared values, code of honor, and ethics unite all men into "bands of brothers," which span vast oceans of space and time. Their folktales, songs, and eyewitness accounts are represented in every culture and every religion throughout written history. It is not our intent to chronical the immensity of this history. Nor do we need yet another book hyping the life of someone you will never meet. It is our goal however to deconstruct the fabric that connects and weaves thousands of years of tradition, across the entirety of the globe, into a clear, concise strategy, so we men may follow in the same footsteps of these giants. We need never again live vicariously through anyone else's life.

To become the men we were intended to be, we must first wake from the fairy tale and the deep dream we have been stuck in since birth. Your perception of your "self" is not real, no matter how painful or glorious that existence may be. You are living in a construct, created over the span of your life. This construct is an accumulation of the thoughts, ideas, and beliefs we hold on to as truths, but which are actually false illusions that play like a movie in our minds, with ourselves as the lead actor.

We all create a personal narrative in our minds. Our "story" acts as a defense system, compartmentalizing life into bite-sized pieces and helping us cope with the perpetual, apparent chaos of a universe we cannot comprehend with just our five senses.

This window of experiencing reality is called "dual consciousness" or *ego*. Its equal opposite, *"non-dual consciousness,"* is the "secret sauce" of all mystical traditions. The dual-consciousness experience (fallen state) is a way of seeing the universe in which you and all other things are separate from one another. We define ourselves by what we are and what we are not, to include our material possessions, afflictions, and the addictions we accumulate through life like hoarders gone mad at a two-for-one flea market. This conscious experience is in and of itself the "fall from grace" and the very obstacle that keeps us stuck in suffering and unable to reach our true potential.

This realization comes with great responsibility and a moment of terror as the "false self" has finally been exposed. First Corinthians 13:11 (NIV) speaks to the heart of our dilemma. *"When I was a child, I talked like a child, I thought like a child, I reasoned like a child. When I became a man, I put the ways of childhood behind me."*

No longer can we blame God, Satan, the universe, Karma, government, our jobs, wives, kids, or even our parents for our personal suffering and shortcomings as men. No longer can we afford to waste our lives and the precious time afforded us by feeding and growing the hungry beast inside with any of the comforts or sinful desires it uses to keep us shackled to our inadequacies and delusions of the "false self." You are not alone in this fight, nor are you powerless or incapable of making the most profound transformation.

We have within us the genetic code of our Warrior ancestry who overcame the very same battle we find ourselves in now. Like it or not, we are in a war. This war will be fought until the Maker Himself declares it won. We have the tools, knowledge, and wisdom of those who came before. The greatest sin of all would be to disregard their sacrifice and slip back into the comatose nature of pervasive darkness we inherited from our primate cousins, primordial man, and Satan himself.

We have access to incredible weaponry and the armor of God, should we choose to don it. We have an immense historical account, a road map of sorts, detailing the lives, acts, and heroism handed down to us by our Warrior ancestors. It is my personal belief born from fifty years of pain and suffering, trial and error, and the endless quest for union with our Maker, that there is no greater Warrior and no greater representation of what we as men should aspire to be than Jesus Christ.

In less than three years, the teachings of Jesus of Nazareth resulted in His persecution, torture, and crucifixion, which literally split time in half. His short life was so powerful we now communicate time and history in terms of Before Christ, "BC," and Anno Domini (the year of our Lord), "AD.".

The martyrdom of Christ and the resurrection that followed spontaneously ignited a movement that has spanned the last two- thousand years, touched the lives of countless generations and reached all four corners of the globe.

I am often asked by friends and family, slowly peeling back the curtains for themselves, "Do you believe in God?" "Do you believe in Jesus Christ and His resurrection?" The answer to that question always brings me to tears due to its profound implications.

Before any of us answers these questions, we should first ask ourselves:

- If I truly "believe" in the existence of God and the resurrection of His Son, why do I continue to live my life in a way that is completely void of the immense implications statements like this merit?

- How do I say I believe in God and Jesus Christ yet continue to live a life of sin?

- How can I believe in the Grand Weaver and His Son when I live a life addicted to material possessions and the desires of my earthly flesh?

- How can I believe in such majesty, yet stay stuck in a life of suffering and separateness fueled by egoic delusions that keep me shackled and deprived of my true potential?"

• Do I truly "believe" or is something still lacking?

So many Christians default to a dogma of shared ideas and belief systems that are shallow at best and fail to reach the contemplative experience we should all strive for when pondering the Gospel. If you believe there is a God, do your actions reflect the enormous responsibility of your belief?

Do you say you believe in God, yet only offer Him an hour of your precious time on Sundays, conveniently somewhere between 10 and noon at your local church?

God is not *convenient*, nor does He respond to your selfish, broken nature. He is not a Happy Meal complete with a set of Ginsu knives you can purchase in three easy installments of $9.95. He is not something you put on the back shelf just in case you need Him one day. Do you say you believe in God but live in judgement of others whom He created? Do you believe in God, but live in sin and attachment to your five senses, a slave to comfort? Do you believe in God but live in fear of your fellow man, his governments, the future, and your inevitable death? Do you believe in God but deface His temple with fast food, alcohol, and drugs?

Many believe in Jesus Christ but take no action to live the life of sacrifice and service He clearly taught. Many believe in Jesus Christ but believe He was a living God, not flesh and blood. If He was a living God, then he could not be the blood seed of Adam, Abraham and David and could not serve as the Goel, the "Kinsmen redeemer" prophesied in the Old Testament. His actions would have been those of an immortal, and we, as flesh and blood, could never rise to meet His expectation that we should "Deny yourself and follow me." To believe that His passion and suffering were somehow diminished because He was divine is to squash His dream and vision for us all. Jesus was God incarnate, but he was also flesh, bone & blood. As such, He suffered unknowable pain & endured the relentless addictions of the flesh. But where Adam failed, Jesus prevailed.

> *"Who, as He already existed in the form of God,*
> *did not consider equality with God something to*
> *be grasped, but emptied Himself by taking the*
> *form of a bond-servant and being made in the*
> *likeness of man. And being found in appearance*
> *as a man, He humbled Himself by becoming*
> *obedient to the point of death: death on a cross"*
> (Philippians 2: 6-8).

My prayer is that each of us will deepen ourselves in Christ, and become the fertile soil, receiving the seed He planted 2000 years ago, living inside us all. That seed is restless, desperately trying to sprout and blossom into the fruit promised us by the Son of Man.

I pray that each one who reads these words accepts the immense responsibility of the Warrior tradition, its passage into manhood, and to finally live as the giants we were intended to be.

PART TWO

THE FIVE PILLARS OF A WARRIOR

CHAPTER FIVE

What Makes a Warrior?

"A Warrior does not give up what he loves,
he finds the love in what he does."
— Dan Millman, author,

Way of the Peaceful Warrior

I f we analyze historical records of the Warrior tradition, our first insight would be to recognize the commonalities all Warriors have shared since written records began, across all corners of the globe. Although the times, geography, technology, tactics, and weapons of choice may change, the substance never does. It is critical for us to thoroughly examine this timeless relationship as one interconnected story that continues today. I see the Warrior saga as an interconnected fabric that penetrates time and space. Every fabric has a core or a central thread that runs throughout.

This being the case, and given the greatest historical accounts and the heroes whose lives and conquests have become immortal, what would you say their most basic commonalities or threads are? Think David to Achilles. King Arthur to General Patton, Chief Tecumseh to the greatest Samurai of all time, Miyamoto Musashi. Countless hardships, strife, and suffering befall our heroes, and we read about the personal means by which they overcome them. Therefore, suffering and pain might be the logical answer and are indeed shared traits, but they are not exclusive to the Warrior class. Suffering is divine and therefore inherent in every life form from amoeba to human.

What is it that makes the Warrior tradition exclusive and elusive to the rest of humanity? Quite simply, it isn't that Warriors do not face the same struggles as the rest of us; they do. It is not the *what* that makes them so different. It is *how* they overcome these obstacles and why. From my vantage point, I have gleaned that there are five principles that reveal themselves throughout history no matter the time, place, culture, or religion. I refer to these principles as the Five Pillars.

The Five Pillars of a Warrior are the Mind, Spirit, Heart, Body, and Skill. These Pillars are the essence of the Warrior. They separate the Warrior from the rest of humanity and unite all Warrior traditions in timeless brotherhood.

Without gaining mastery over our minds, we can never move on to the higher states of consciousness found in the Warrior Spirit. To cultivate the Warrior Spirit requires a daily practice where one looks death squarely in the face and wholly accepts its promise for us all. As Warriors mature and deepen their understanding of death, they begin to come to terms with and lose the inherited fear that has gripped the minds and paralyzed the bodies of our ancestors since death was first experienced.

As fear subsides, wisdom and freedom fill the void once occupied by fear. Universal truths become exposed. The first truth is that death is not the end of anything other than our own ego or persona. Our persona (Latin for *mask*) or "false self" is at the heart of all fears. Stemming from this concept of ego, the Bodhisattva describes four basic fears we all share:

- death

- sickness

- poverty

- old age

Fear is the ego's resistance to what is. Fear is never in the present, but always in the future, always in anxious expectation. This means our egos are hardwired to not accept change in any other form other than the kind of change the ego wants or expects. This egoic resistance is the root of all suffering. The practice of letting go of attachment to all things, including our very lives, gives rise to our spiritual awakening.

Nothing Dies — Everything Transforms

> **"No matter how hard the past, you can always begin again."**
> **—Buddha**

Change, or transformation, is the very footprint of God's creation and our most fundamental essence. There is nothing permanent in the universe (Genesis 3). Everything, every galaxy, solar system, star, planet, mineral, bacteria, and animal is interconnected and interdependent upon each other and absolutely impermanent. No "thing" stands alone. Only God is *intra*-dependent, not relying on anything else for His existence. He is perfect in Himself alone. All else, including you and me, is in a constant state of flux or transformation.

The reality of our universe and the divine creation is that whatever is born dies, and is reborn in every moment or "now" in what our ego refers to as *time*. Time is only one of the four dimensions man exists (height, width, depth, time) out of at least ten dimensions currently known to exist. Time is also a construct man has created in his exhaustive attempt to resist and control what is. Time does not exist anywhere other than the imagination of man and the lower dimensions of his existence and conciousness.

The pure ferocity and speed by which God creates cannot be understood by our finite minds nor dualistic ego. This is only possible through years of contemplation, meditation, the dropping of our egos, and the cultivation of non-dualistic consciousness. Over *time*, we become so porous that the truth of the universe and therefore the divinity of the Creator can become manifest in our newly gained perception.

Through the Warrior Spirit we face our fears, strike them down with the sword of our consciousness, and come to know our true selves. Through the Warrior Heart, we do not avoid the abyss but, instead, leap into it headfirst.

Using this newly gained insight, the Warrior can clearly see without judgement or prejudice that which makes him both human and being. Our experience of the universe and our ability to relate with it is reliant on the four energies we all share but, again, are magnified to their fullest potential by the Warrior tradition. They are:

- Physical

- Mental

- Emotional

- Spiritual

The Warrior knows he is not a physical body with a soul; he is a soul with a physical body. Through divine intelligent design, we have been blessed with a massive brain capable of more than every supercomputer on the planet. We have not only five senses but a sixth, often referred to as ESP (extra-sensory perception), and a seventh—the ability to understand and dwell in the principles that underly the universe (Natural law). The Warrior consumes his days with skillset acquisition. He hardens and strengthens his body. He learns to use his body as a finely tuned instrument. After performing thousands upon thousands of repetitions, his body finally, in and of itself, becomes his weapon of choice.

The Warrior craves knowledge and never stops learning. He is a perpetual student constantly refining, educating, and exploring the depths of his mind. He learns to "feel" and then consciously let go of every and all emotion, as opposed to shoving them down or acting as if he were free of such nonsense. Instead, he learns to master emotion and wield it as a tool or weapon when and where needed. Lastly, he lives in the *now* and, as such, lives life to its fullest potential, cradled in the arms of God.

In his pursuit, the Warrior realizes his true purpose: the loving, fostering protection of all life.

His sacrifice is not for himself but for a greater good.

CHAPTER SIX

THE WARRIOR MIND

"If you die before you die, then when you die,
you will not die."

—Words written above the Gateway at St. Paul's
Monastery, Mt. Athos, Greece

There are two legendary figures who are so synonymous with Warrior mindset that they border on cliché. They are the Spartan Warriors of ancient Greece and the Japanese samurai.

From age seven to adulthood, all Spartan men, except the firstborn of the ruling class, were expected to attend the infamous *Agoge*, the Spartan Warrior school. According to Plutarch, the main purpose of the *Agoge* was for Spartan boys to undergo intense physical trials to prepare their bodies for the harshness of war. The boys were routinely beaten, treated like animals, and subjected to years of brutality. By age twelve, boys were expected to steal food and were underfed to inspire this behavior. Ironically, if the boys were caught in the act, they were brutally punished—not for stealing, but for getting caught. It was thought that this created resourcefulness, cunning, and

69

stealth in the young Warriors. Nothing was overlooked to harden Spartan children. They wrestled, worked, exposed themselves to the harshness of the burning Greek sun, and even slept on tough reeds sewn together from the Eurotas River.

The Agoge empowered young Spartan boys with a deeply convicted sense of duty and moral code. Conformity, unity, courage, patriotism, martial prowess, guile, and brutality were driven into every ounce of flesh. All in the name of Sparta. Upon adulthood, these boys served in the Spartan army and were expected to fight in all military campaigns. They were, however, also free to marry, have families, and own land.

There is no doubt amongst historians that the sheer ferocity of the Spartan Warrior was totally founded in the Agoge. The ancient Greeks were not only brilliant thinkers, artisans, and builders, they also knew the cost of their free state came at the price of blood that was shed by the few men able to spill it.

We should never minimize the bravery or sheer grit it took to wage war with bladed weapons — or how important this ability still is today. The battlefields of the ancient world were fought man to man and face to face. Only a few surviving veterans from the island campaigns of World War II, and bloody hand-to-hand engagements in Korea and Viet Nam can express the madness and sheer chaos of what a Spartan soldier must have experienced in war. Imagine the battlefield. Sounds of metal on metal, men screaming in pain and grunting in unison, plowing into the enemy with their shields. The dense iron smells of blood, comingling with fear-filled sweat, urine, and feces, covering the ground, turning it to dank, slippery muck. Men falling, crawling, and clawing through the filth over their dead brothers, trying to gain enough purchase of ground to thrust one more blade into the belly of another human being.

Ending a man's life and taking from him all he ever was and all he would ever be.

In The Unforgiven, Clint Eastwood's character says, "Killing is a hell of a thing." He's right.

I refer to Lt. Colonel Dan Grossman's books ("On Killing: The Psychological Cost of Learning to Kill in War and Society" and "On Combat, The Psychology and Physiology of Deadly Conflict in War and in Peace") several times in this chapter and recommend you read all material written by Grossman. Colonel Grossman is the leading researcher on the Warrior mindset with special consideration being given to the central causation of Post-Traumatic Stress Disorder (PTSD) and the skill acquisition involved in training young soldiers how to kill their own kind.

Grossman's books go into considerable detail concerning the connection of PTSD with the "inter-personal" level of combat experienced by the soldier. For instance, rarely do fighter pilots, artillery specialists, or even drone pilots, suffer from symptoms of trauma related to a combat experience. In stark contrast, more than forty percent of all discharges from the military during World War II were related to the infantry suffering from "combat fatigue." During the Viet Nam conflict, thirty percent of the soldiers returning home were thought to have suffered symptoms of PTSD. Roughly twenty percent of Afghanistan and Iraq war veterans showed signs of PTSD, though I believe that number to be much higher.

One contributing factor Grossman offers is the level of fear, or terror, and subsequent trauma related to the level of inter-personal conflict a soldier experiences with the enemy he is charged to kill, as well as the distance at which he slays said enemy. While I am not minimizing the hardship or necessity of gaining the skies as high ground in combat, fighter pilots rarely, if ever, see the death and destruction caused by their missiles and bombs. The same is true for artillery, drone pilots, and naval bombardment.

Death from the sky, as delivered by the U.S. military, is the most devastating force ever devised. However, in order to hold physical territory, a soldier (a Warrior) with a rifle or a blade must be positioned on the ground. When you choose to do this, at some point that individual is going to have to get up close and personal with the enemy, look into his eyes, and snuff out his life.

The brutal truth is absolutely required when discussing the realities of self-defense and the potential necessity of taking the life of an attacker. The rose-colored glasses a potential sheepdog may tend to wear when regarding the taking of another life should be stomped out of existence. Even the most skilled operators will come to terms with the harsh reality that the enemy was also a human being, not just a target whose death was justified. Only psychopaths, sociopaths, or someone burying their trauma will not feel remorse or reflect on these deeds with some level of regret. At some point, they will be forced to unpack this trauma psychologically and spiritually.

I have met many veterans who have lost a piece of themselves to the harshness of their combat experiences. I include myself in their number. Sometimes Warriors must become so hardened they lose a piece of their souls forever. In this pit of hell, it seems like a giant abyss is swallowing us whole, with no escape in sight. More than 6,000 suicides a year have occurred since 2008 as a result of the brutality of war and the lingering trauma left untreated. Having been there myself, my hypothesis of what is causing this trauma is threefold. And its remedy is its complete opposite.

- **Problem:** Lack of realistic mental preparation regarding the brutality of warfare, with special attention placed on inter-personal, face-to-face combat.

  Solution: Prioritizing and desensitizing Warriors to reality of conflict and inter-personal combat with real-world training modalities and environments, pressure testing, and education while inducing "Flow State." I will discuss this state in detail within the next few pages.

- **Problem:** Lack of immediate psychological unpacking and spiritual reconciliation.

  Solution: Warriors should conduct daily, after-action reviews of their activities in the field during both combat and training to include any and all emotions, thoughts, or physical or psychological anomalies that may have occurred.

Warriors should be educated regarding the normal physiological and psychological effects that accompany high-stress environments and combat, such as wetting one's pants. Warriors or victims of any trauma should never be allowed to internalize feelings of shame, guilt, or cowardice in association with something completely natural.

The reality is that no matter how much we train, we can never know how much of us will show up to the fight and how much of us will hide in a closet. There is no normal in combat. There is only the experience of the moment that needs to be individualized, objectified, and unpacked, so the soldier does not internalize the trauma.

- **Problem:** Lack of a true moral or existential threat to the life of the Warrior, citizens, and loved ones.

  Solution: From a military standpoint, elected officials should only use our military forces after all peaceful means of conflict resolution have taken place. Given this, no deployment of military arsenal or forces should be used for any reason other than self-defense or an existential threat to our nation and its peoples. From a civilian standpoint, the same rules should apply. Lethal force should be avoided at all costs, and if non-lethal means of conflict resolution are available, they must be taken. It is morally or legally acceptable to dispense an evil doer in situations of self-defense or those threatening the lives of loved ones or citizens whom we protect.

We can never minimize the necessity of training in the "Suck," combined with increasing tolerances of pain and suffering. As modern men living in a modern "soft" culture, this process is harder than ever to replicate or create. Therefore, periodic, high levels of stress need to be placed on the physical body. This can be implemented through hours of heavy, arduous, lactic-acid-filled physical exercise, and/or consistent martial arts training (especially in grappling arts). Consider the possibility of cultivating a mindset along the way that could single-handedly remedy the psychological and spiritual wounds of combat before they take place. What if this mindset could propel us to superhuman performance levels?

That psychological state does exist. We call it the "Flow State" or "Flow Consciousness."

For centuries, samurai Warriors of ancient Japan wrestled with the same issues as Warriors of today. They did not fight with F-18s or drones flown from Las Vegas, but with exquisitely sharp, three-foot razor blades capable of cutting a man in half with one fell swoop. Text upon text was written by these ancient samurai, but few had anything to do with skill acquisition. Samurai seemed not the least bit concerned with the physical technique of swordsmanship. Instead, their efforts were spent cultivating the mind of the Warrior in the heat of battle. Their preferred method for obtaining this mindset was the intense study of Zen Buddhism and hours upon hours of meditation. In the truest sense of irony, this pursuit not only made the samurai the greatest, most lethal Warriors ever to walk the planet, but also the most spiritually enlightened. Their preferred teachers were not master swordsmen but enlightened monks. Among them, none were more prophetic or in tune with the psychological and spiritual requirements of the samurai Warrior than Takuan Soho.

CHAPTER SEVEN

The Warrior Spirit

"For God so loved the world that He gave His only
begotten Son, that whoever believes in Him
should not perish but have everlasting life"
(John 3:16).

A thousand years before His birth, sages predicted the Messiah would come. The Old Testament concealed what the New Testament revealed. God Himself, our Creator, would walk among us and spill His blood for the sake of His lost children. His sacrifice caused Heaven and Earth to stand still, as absolutes (love, justice, evil, and forgiveness) collided into a singularity of hope. A second birth of humanity. A spiritual Big Bang—and a chance for us all to right the wrongs of our ancestors.

Without the Crucifixion there is no gospel. Without the gospel, there is no grace. Where there is no grace, there is no faith. Where there is no faith, there is only darkness.

Christianity is the only worldview that has both a divine instruction manual (the Holy Bible) and, more importantly, a perfect, living example of God's image of man—the *Son of*

God and Son of Man, Jesus Christ. Where Adam failed, Jesus prevailed.

Christianity is the only worldview where the promise of redemption, transformation, and eternal life of our souls is **not** won by our good deeds outweighing the bad (*Karma*), but by faith and grace alone. There is *nothing* we can do in our fallen state to right the terrible wrongs of the original sin we inherited through Adam and Eve, our ancient parents. Nothing.

The only way to lift this curse is through the Gospel of Jesus Christ, freely given to His believers by the most incredible, selfless act of love and forgiveness in history: the Crucifixion.

Along with this tremendous gift, Jesus also lays an immense responsibility at our feet. In Mark 8:34 (NKJV) He tells us, *"Whoever desires to come after Me, let him deny himself, and take up his cross, and follow Me."* We must also live by faith in the Son of God, not merely say the words. This means we must put all faith in Him, face our inner demons and fears, let go of egoic selfish ways, forgo our addictions to the flesh, and dwell in Him and Him alone. Jesus wants us to live lives of truth and be willing to accept the consequences as did countless Christian martyrs throughout history.

Faith in Jesus Christ requires that we nail ourselves to the cross by the sacrifice we make every day for the good of humanity and the betterment of His Church. Jesus' desire is that we leave our lives of comfort and the sins of our flesh and walk unwaveringly through the fires of hell into the suffering of our fallen brothers and sisters. *"Follow Me"* means to live by faith and become a Warrior of the light in fervent service to your friends, family, neighborhood, city, state, and nation.

"Very truly I tell you, whoever believes in me will do the works I have been doing, and they will do even greater things

than these, because I am going to the Father. And I will do whatever you ask in my name, so that the Father may be glorified in the Son" (John 14:12-13).

Living in Trinity

The Gospel itself is a Trinitarian concept, as shown in John 14:6 (NIV). Jesus tells us, *"I am the way, the truth, and the life."*

First, there is an Initiation: *"I am the way."*

We cannot save ourselves. We must have a teacher and a direct transmission of grace through Jesus and Jesus *alone*. This initiation is the physical speaking of the words of the Gospel. No matter your current standing in Christ, please follow along, speaking these words aloud and from your heart, choosing every day to take Jesus Christ as your personal Teacher, Lord, and Savior.

"I believe

- *Jesus is the "Logos," the Creator Himself incarnated in the flesh as a human man.*

- *He was born of a virgin and was free of original sin.*

- *He is the blood seed of Abraham and the rightful King of Israel prophesied by the ancient saints.*

- *He lived a sinless life.*

- *He died on the cross as a blood sacrifice, embodying our sins that we may be redeemed.*

- *He was entombed in the earth for three days.*

79

- *He defeated death and rose from the grave, walking among us for forty days.*

- *He ascended into heaven and will return for His Church.*

This initiation creates relationship with Jesus as our personal, ever-present Teacher, Savior, and Lord. This relationship deepens throughout our lives, as we grow in Him and lose ourselves in His Gospel.

Secondly, there is Transformation. "*I am... the truth.*"

Through the gospels, we follow Jesus and carry our own crosses. We consciously move into our suffering and explore its roots and transformative gifts. We then nail ourselves to the cross and die to our lives of suffering and sin through the re-birth of our souls in Christ. We are now risen from the dead to live eternally from this point forth, forever in His presence, ambassadors of Christ on Earth and in Heaven.

Third, we have Salvation: "*I am... the Life.*" Without Jesus' selfless act on the cross, we are all doomed to a life of suffering in our fallen state. Through His sacrifice we may live eternally in His presence, becoming His joy and His glory on Earth and in Heaven.

The Trinity Defined

"*In the beginning was the Word, and the Word was with God, and the Word was God*" *(John 1:1).*

The basis of the Trinity is that God is three equal persons. One God. One being. Three equal entities—Father, Son, and Holy Spirit (mind, body & soul).

The Father is absolute *form-less-ness.* He is perfectly intra-dependent and thus perfect. Omnipotent. Omniscient.

Omnipresent. He is pure love, pure potentiality. Pure consciousness and utterly empty of form.

The second person is the Son, or the *Logos* (Word) who was incarnated in the physical body of Jesus Christ. The Son is the originator of all realms of creation to include Heaven and Earth, and thus all *form* is of His body. This includes the unlimited variations of form as it arises, both physical and non-physical, in Heaven and the universe we perceive as reality.

The third person of the Trinity is the Holy Spirit. The Holy Spirit is the force that permeates every subatomic particle in the universe and every angelic body in Heaven, interconnecting all creation in unified purpose. Paul writes in Corinthians 6:19, *"Do you not know that your bodies are temples of the Holy Spirit, who is in you, whom you have received from God? You are not your own."*

Though there are three seemingly separate entities, Father, Son, and Holy spirit, they are One in actuality.

All of us, at some point, have felt the presence of the Holy Spirit. Without Him we are just subatomic soup lacking God's will and His obvious grand design. Even in our fallen state the Holy Spirit is within us, just inaccessible. It was the Father's intention that his Son would create life on Earth to include human beings, formed in *our* image (*Genesis*). Human beings who could (through Christ) become conscious of consciousness itself, living in perfect Union with the Triune God.

The Holy Bible teaches us that, since Adam's fall into a life of sin, Man perpetually stumbles and fails. We can be led out of perpetual darkness and into the light of His grand design through the birth, death, and resurrection of Jesus Christ, Son of Man, Son of God, the *"Messiah"* promised throughout scripture and sent by our Father. Jesus, the Lamb of God, the perfect example of what Man was always intended to be, was sent to Earth for one purpose: to become sin and to spill His blood so we may finally be redeemed. This powerful realization is the heart and soul of the Gospel or the "Good News."

The promise of eternal life can only be gained through our wholehearted acceptance of the saving grace afforded to us through faith in Christ. With our new standing in Christ and our study of and adherence to scripture, we begin to grasp the reality of God's infinite love for us. Through the Word and the prompting of the indwelling Holy Spirit, the Father guides and interjects His will for the benefit of His majestic creation.

The gravity of this loving act and its implications should leave us speechless. Its enormity is the sole basis for the prerequisite of Christian faith. God sent His only Son to awaken us from perpetual darkness and separateness from him. He sent the Messiah to lift us from a life of sin and awaken us to the everlasting light of His Kingdom. Awakened to truth and a conscious experience that all life — in all forms, in Heaven and Earth, in its endless wonders — is One and this Oneness is the totality of God Himself.

This concept of Oneness, which is referred to throughout St. Paul's epistles, is not just solid Christian theology, but is a transformative mystical experience accessible to all believers.

Paul writes in Galatians 3:26-28, *"So in Christ Jesus you are all children of God through faith, for all you who were baptized into Christ have clothed yourself with Christ. There is neither Jew nor Gentile, neither slave nor free, nor is there male and female, for you are all one in Christ Jesus."*

The term *Christ* is derived from the ancient Greek word *Christos*, meaning *"anointed one."* Christ's body constitutes every subatomic particle in the universe and our concept of reality. Christ is the *Logos* comprising Heaven, angelic bodies, the cosmos, the sky, oceans, animals, plants, and even our thoughts and dreams. The Body of Christ is one interconnected *nowness* in constant transformation, as revealed by the ancient Celtics through the knots they carved into stone crosses built around the eighth century. These crosses can be found in the lands of Ireland, France, and England to this day.

To truly embrace the essence of Christianity one must understand that everyone, everything, and every *now*, in our experience of reality is sacred. Both Jesus of Nazareth and His mystic Apostle Paul repeatedly point to this powerful realization throughout the New Testament. Paul writes in Ephesians 3:8-9"

"To me, the very least of all the holy ones, this grace was given, to preach to the Gentiles the inscrutable riches of Christ, and to bring to light what is the plan of the mystery hidden from ages past in God who created all things."

The Holy Trinity and the teachings of Jesus are impossible to truly grasp through dual-consciousness or a state of mind in which everything, including us, is separate. There is *me*, a construct of the ego, and *every-thing* else. The Trinity is our first awakening that our logical, analytical, and judgmental ways of thinking are utterly bankrupt of spiritual awareness. Neither the five senses nor the egoic binary filter we pour the entirety of the universe through is capable of comprehending the majesty of God's Kingdom.

The proof of this is buried deep inside the commandment Jesus heralded as the commandment second only to loving the Lord your God with all your heart, soul, and mind, "Love your neighbor as yourself" (Matthew 22:39). Jesus is telling us in no uncertain terms that through our broken dual-conscious experience we *see* our neighbors as separate, different. Through this difference we construct a constant, false sense of ourselves and the universe.

Jesus is telling us is that our neighbor *is* us, that we are all *one*. One consciousness. One nowness arising for the moment in human form. Through the use of parables, Jesus attempts to dislodge our ego's broken perception of ourselves and awaken the non-dual Christ consciousness inside us all.

Ego

To achieve Christ consciousness, we must stop looking to the outside for answers and go deeper inside. Inside our DNA lies the footprint of God. Contained in every mitochondrion (the central computer of the cell) is the universal library of every life form ever to have existed on planet Earth. The mitochondria are the epicenter for the eternal voice that speaks to us all. We refer to this voice as our conscience, but it is none other than the voice of God Himself in the form of the Holy Spirit.

Few of us pay attention to this voice. Fewer act on it. Our busy lives and modern society have wedged a monster-sized chasm between our hearts and the endless other voices and thoughts churning in our minds. This relentless internal chatter is referred to in Zen Buddhism as "monkey mind." The monkey mind is an unconscious construct of the ego that uses thought forms to process the complexities of the universe and to keep us separate and asleep from our true selves.

According to Carl Jung, the *self* is enormously complex. Jung lists a minimum of a dozen phenomenon that compile the self to include:

- the outer physical world

- projections

- persona

- archetypes

- personal consciousness

- ego

- shadow

- personal unconsciousness

- anima/animus

- collective unconsciousness

To use Jung's terms, we can think of the collective unconscious as the totality of all souls—past, present, and future—to include all knowledge and the infinite wisdom of the cosmos.

This collective unconsciousness is the inner voice of our ancestral fathers that speaks to us, especially in times of strife and suffering. The self is a sort of gathering place, or collection center, for all information both internal and external and is as malleable as clay. The ego is the relatively miniscule component of the self that is created from life experiences, thought forms, beliefs, and minute amounts of content that seep through from the collective unconscious to the personal consciousness.

Both our concepts of self and the ego are literally erased or washed clean (*tabula rasa*) upon our verbal proclamation (*initiation*) of the true Gospel, along with a deepening level of living faith. This is the Christian experience of being *born again.* Jesus clearly makes a point of this during his late-night discussion with Nicodemus. *"Jesus answered and said unto him, Verily, verily, I say unto thee, Except a man be born again, he cannot see the kingdom of God"* (John 3:3 KJV).

The "shadow" separates the ego from the massive collective unconscious. The easiest way to grasp the context of the shadow is to see it arising in other people. How many angry people hate and despise angry people? How many people live a life of sloth but cannot stand lazy people? The shadow is a construct inside the self that keeps us, or our egos, from realizing or seeing certain elements of ourselves. This construct, which are nothing less than prison gates, locks us into a life of suffering, pain, separateness, and unconsciousness. Sin is the vehicle the shadow uses to wage war on the *true self.* The ancient Greeks defined sin, a term used by archers, as "to miss the mark or bullseye." The Roman Catholic Church categorizes what it calls deadly sins into seven categories:

- lust

- gluttony

- greed

- sloth

- wrath

- envy

- pride

St. John of the Cross writes in his Magnus Opus, "The Ascent of Mt. Carmel," that the pathway to union with God is a precarious walk on the razor's edge of life.

On both sides of this razor's edge lies the abyss and the eternal dark side. John teaches that one must attain single-minded focus to attain union with God. To reach this summit, one must first suffer the "dark night of the soul."

This dark night is the experience of the self as it suffers through the loss of the senses and addictions, much akin to the melancholy that accompanies the death of a family member or loved one. The dark night is a purging or cleansing of the self from the addictions of the five senses and the attachment to all earthly forms that precedes union with our heavenly Father. It is through the sheer reliance of faith and the grace of God that one navigates this tumultuous path, so we may once again find ourselves in the arms of our Father and our true selves.

Coincidentally, we find the same conclusion and remarkably similar aesthetic in the monastic practices shared by mystics at all four corners of the globe. Somehow, over thousands of years, they each came to the same conclusions pertaining to spirituality without knowing the other existed. Over 2600 years ago, Siddhartha Gautama, the Buddha, which means enlightened one, founded one of today's four major spiritual traditions (Christianity, Judaism, Islam, and Buddhism).

Buddhism is not a religion. It is a means of training the mind and attaining right mindedness, so we may see reality as it truly is. At its core, the Buddha teaches us that all life is suffering. We suffer due to our shared resistance of what is. From birth, we are born into suffering. According to Buddha, suffering's major causality is the formation of the ego and its massive resistance to the oneness of God's universe, in addition to the endless separation of itself through the attachment to form and the ceaseless constructs of the mind and a life of sin. Isn't this a powerful description of our fallen state?

Every mystical tradition on our planet, including the teachings of Jesus Christ and His apostles, teaches the same things about suffering:

- Suffering is a divine byproduct of life.

- Suffering is caused by the rise of man's ego.

- Man's ego creates attachment.

- Attachment creates more suffering.

- To end suffering, man must do battle with his own ego and its attachments to the five senses and earthly forms.

- Once awakened, man's suffering ends as he experiences union with God and the Oneness of His universe.

That is the *what*. The *how* can be found by grace alone. It is not my goal to highlight other world religions or beliefs. My point in discussing other religious beliefs is that all human creation on earth intuitively grasps the essence of our fallen state and the endless cycle of suffering. While other religions may offer enlightenment into our shared fallen state, only the grace of God through faith in Jesus Christ can free us from the chains of this hellish burden. All inhabitants of Earth have been offered this gift freely given through the Gospel of Jesus Christ and the power of His written word. The Five Solas, which distinguished the tenets of the Reformation from the teachings of the Roman Catholic Church are:

By grace alone.
Through faith alone.
In Christ alone.
According to Scripture alone.
For the glory of God alone.

Our resistance to Christ consciousness is the epicenter of our suffering and the seemingly impenetrable wall that separates us from our Heavenly Father, His Son, and Holy Spirit. The spiritual journey of the ancient saints is a rocky, chaotic road filled with obstacles, cavernous valleys, and seemingly unscalable mountains. In his book, W*hat's Wrong with the World,* Christian theologian G.K. Chesterton states, *"The Christian ideal has not been tried and found wanting; it has been found difficult and left untried."*

The only true way to take this journey and arrive at our divine destination is to take the straightest, narrowest path, and walk the razor's edge, as presented by John of the Cross and countless enlightened saints and apostles before and after him.

The razor's edge is the Warrior's path. It is a monastic pursuit requiring intense prayer, meditation, and a resolution to rid the self of all attachment to the addictions of the flesh and all earthly things. This path leads those who are brave enough to make the arduous journey to the attainment and conscious realization of *no self* and the great awakening that we are *One* in the Body of Christ.

CHAPTER EIGHT

THE WARRIOR HEART

"I shake my head like a wet dog, start to low-crawl and yell for the boys to follow. Within minutes, I am moving so fast, I lose track of my team. Something has shifted in me. The fear is gone. Doubt and paralysis are gone. All replaced by a euphoric sense of calm acceptance and a surge of what I can only describe as boundless energy. Years of training in the suck has rewired my brain and body. Self-pity and agony are just triggering now. Once pulled, they unleash the beast. They are no longer an excuse to quit. This option no longer exists in my nervous system.

"I reach the top of a ridge and quickly roll over the other side for cover. As my team continues to maneuver under fire, we start setting up a perimeter, return fire as best we can, and wait for the rest of the company to arrive. As I look around, it is a horrible sight. Troopers everywhere are dropping like flies. Several have been shot or injured by shrapnel, and at least half of us are circling the drain, borderline unconscious from heat stroke."

— Stewart Breeding, *Biohacker* 2017

The Individual Will

> *"Strength does not come from physical capacity.*
> *It comes from an indomitable will."*
> *—Mahatma Gandhi*

Immediately following the Airborne operation to seize the Torrijos International Airport outside of Panama City in 1989, my unit (Bravo Company 1/504th 82nd Airborne) was tasked to do an air assault outside of Panama City to secure a mountaintop objective being held by several hundred Special Operations forces from the remaining PDF (Panamanian Defense Force). As we hovered above the Landing Zone (LZ), the choppers came under fire from small arms, mortars, and snipers. We were getting shot up so badly we had no choice but to jump out of the choppers hovering some twenty feet over the LZ, in the middle of the enemy's kill zone, each of us loaded with over 100 pounds of gear.

From the second my body slammed into the ground, I was bombarded by flying dirt and debris, exploding everywhere from the impact of bullets and mortars being fired from every direction imaginable.

There is no way to describe the incapacitating terror that grips the entirety of your being during the first moments of combat. My personal experience was one of extreme polarity that changed my life forever. On one side, I was seized by complete and total paralyses caused by the sonic vibrations in the air. The bullets buzzed around me like hornets, each one coming within millimeters of ending my life.

On the other side, I experienced the most tremendous, euphoric, extraordinary sensation, as my body, mind, and spirit merged into one collaborative effort beyond something super-human. I laid with my head in the dirt, trying to see how small I could make myself. If I didn't start moving, if I didn't swallow my fear and the tremendous amounts of suck being dumped on me, my entire unit would die, including me.

As I lay there trying to process the un-processible, something clicked—literally. Gone were my fear and hesitation. Gone were the paralysis, tunnel vision, and egoic concern for my safety. In a fleeting moment, sheer, horrific terror was replaced by a calm, steadfast presence that no longer thought of or feared death.

In that space, I fell back onto my training and the combat tactics that had been deeply planted in my nervous system through thousands of hours of brutal training and my affection for the suck. For the remainder of that bloody, horrible day in which two of our brothers lost their lives, I remained in bliss. I felt no pain. I sensed no fear, no thirst, no hunger. Time stood still and, in the pit of hell, I was more alive than I will ever be again.

I have already spoken extensively about flow and how to achieve this superhuman state of consciousness whenever and wherever you choose. Now, I want to draw your attention to the precursor to flow and the seeds that must be sown prior to unleashing any ultra-states of performance. There are two central ingredients that work together as the hammer and anvil, forging the soul to glimpse the flow state. They are the "suck" and the individual will.

Embrace "The suck"

> *"Accept failure. Enjoy it even.*
> *For the suck is part of the process."*
> **—A.J. Jacobs**

This is the second book I have written in which much attention has been given to the *suck*. We can effectively deduce that this topic is important and warrants a considerable amount of time and thought. The suck is the catalyst for change. It is a better way to describe suffering. The suck is the murky, muddy, poop-filled swamp that produces the exquisitely sublime lotus flower. The suck is the years of practice and tremendous sacrifice an athlete makes to be a champion. The suck is any painful, agonizing, seemingly impossible task or experience one engages in that molds the soul, develops mental grit, and the heart of the Warrior.

To *embrace the suck* means to consciously accept our suffering now, in order to produce a better outcome in the future. This is an enlightened, non-dual way of reasoning and the way of the Warrior. The Warrior never takes the easy way out; he looks for the challenge. He thrives in the presence of adversity. He does not do this for another notch in his cap or yet another beer-time story. He does this because he knows the more suck he endures, the greater the depth of his character, his individual will, and chances of surviving when you-know-what hits the fan.

The *will* is that voice deep inside your gut that refuses to be beaten and will not accept anything other than excellence and your absolute best effort. It is the inner power and outer symbol of manhood you wear proudly on your shoulder. Willpower is the central component of the Warrior Heart. The need for its constant cultivation should never be understated nor underdeveloped.

To my knowledge, there is no greater testament to the power of the individual will and the seemingly untapped superhuman abilities we all possess than the story of Louis "Louie" Zamperini as told in the best-selling novel, *Unbroken*.

After graduating high school, Louie Zamperini won an invitation to compete in the 1936 Berlin Olympics, where he set a world record for the fastest last lap of an Olympic race. As Louie was training for the next Olympic games, the world descended into war. With the Olympic games cancelled due to the outbreak of World War II, Louie enlisted in the Air Force. In 1941, after completing military training, he became a bombardier and was assigned to a military base in the Pacific theatre.

On a routine mission, Louie's plane crashed into the Pacific Ocean. Only Louie and two others survived. The three boarded an inflatable life raft with limited rations, sparse water, and no protection from the hot sun or the sharks constantly stalking them. The men collected rainwater, caught birds to use the meat for fishing, and even managed to kill and eat several sharks. After an astonishing forty-seven days adrift at sea, Louie was finally captured by a passing Japanese military ship and imprisoned.

The Japanese brought Louie to a military base called "Execution Island," where he was placed in a small cage and given little food. Subjected to unspeakable cruelties, he was injected with experimental chemicals and beaten daily. Instead of executing him, the Japanese sent Louie to the Omori labor camp, where one of the head guards, Mutsuhiro "The Bird" Watanabe, singled out Louie for emotional and physical torture. The Japanese were notoriously cruel to war prisoners. Because of Louie's reputation as an Olympic hero, the Bird knew that breaking Louie's will would shatter the entirety of the American POWs remaining moral and fighting spirit.

At one point, Japanese propagandists gave Louie the opportunity to send his family a message over the radio. The U.S. Army had mistakenly announced Louie's death, but his family never lost hope he was still alive. The Japanese broadcasted

Louie's message throughout the U.S., giving his family the first real indication that he was alive. The propagandists told Louie that he could leave the camp and live in a nice hotel, if he agreed to read propaganda on the radio. Louie fought back the only way he could. He refused, and his captors sent him back to the prison camp.

Soon after, the Bird transferred to another POW camp, but, astonishingly, he brought Louie along with him so he could continue the unspeakable abuse. At this camp, Louie hauled tons of coal on his back all day. One day a guard pushed him. Louie slipped and broke his leg and was no longer able to work. The Bird forced Louie to clean out the pig pens instead, while crawling on his hands and knees. This humiliation almost broke Louie's spirit for good, but he was determined to hold on.

In 1945, after more than two years of humiliation and torture, the Japanese suddenly announced the war was over. As U.S. bombers delivered food and clothing to the prisoners, Louie, emaciated and exhausted, knew his freedom was at hand. But days before the war ended, the Bird learned about the impending Japanese surrender and fled the camp, fearing that the Allies would try him as a war criminal. Within days, Louie was freed. After forty-seven days of floating hopelessly on the Pacific Ocean and more than two years of starvation and torture, what was left of Louie finally returned home to his family.

Once home, Louie's torture continued. As you can imagine, he struggled for many years with PTSD, alcoholism, and abuse. Not until a serendipitous revival in his hometown with no other than the Reverend Billy Graham would Louie's story come full circle. After years of "pulling himself up by his bootstraps" and with his own willpower exhausted, Louie surrendered himself freely and wholly to Jesus Christ. Louie would spend the remainder of his days as a Christian evangelist, meeting and forgiving many of his Japanese captors. In 1998 at age 81, he carried the torch at the Winter Olympic Games in Nagano, Japan.

Louie's epic story of courage, strength, and willpower in the face of the most dreadful adversity is one of the single greatest achievements of human endurance on record. His incorruptible integrity and desire to survive was his single source of sustenance for over two years. It replaced water, food, companionship, and purpose. But, in the end, Louie finally succumbed to his tortured mind and depleted soul, as we all do eventually, and hit bottom. Hitting bottom is not a new term for most of us. I imagine you've come to know at least a few "false bottoms" at this point in your life. Just as the suck is a divine, individualized gift from the Almighty, so is your true bottom.

We cannot say enough about the mind-blowing abilities of the human spirit and the sheer individual will to survive in the face of life-threatening adversity. But individual will is finite and, at some point, will be exhausted. At that point, the individual reaches a true bottom where the ego is completely fractured and impossible to reassemble. In this utter brokenness and in the depths of despair, our Heavenly Father waits.

Uniting of Wills. True strength.

My theological beliefs, combined with my personal experience, lead me to the conclusion that the pathway and attainment to union with God is accomplished through these six vehicles:

- Conscious suffering

- Conscious surrender

- Cultivating stillness of the mind

- Eradicating addiction to earthly things

- Loving, fostering protection and service to all sentient creatures

The Desert Fathers and monks across the globe have pursued ascetic traditions for thousands of years — since long before Jesus of Nazareth was born. These traditions include prolonged periods of silence, self-imposed pain and punishment, fasting, fervent prayer, meditation, hallucinogens, solitude, and even dance. These acts are spiritual practices offered by the seeker in desperate, passionate hope to one day glimpse the face of God.

Our heavenly Father will interject Himself in our lives by placing obstacles in front of us. Though we may not realize it at the time, overcoming these obstacles requires the same ascetic process practiced by monks for thousands of years. Let us examine the similarities in Louie's story to the Desert Fathers.

God heaps upon Louie the exact amount of suffering and suck required to break Louie's individual will. No more, no less. Unbeknownst to Louie, as a POW he is forced into a life of extreme ascetic practice. He is starved, beaten, and humiliated. He is removed from society, friends, family, and career. His sense of time, space, and reality are completely distorted. God keeps Louie alive long enough to bring him to his knees because only God knows how far we must go and how much pain we must endure before we finally succumb to His will and let go of our own.

Yes, this process almost killed Louie, but, once again, your level of suffering and the quantity of suck you must endure is personal to you. No two people experience the same amount of suffering, and there is no guarantee that conscious surrender will follow. Sadly, people often cannot see through their pain and terminate this process prematurely. They may do this through addiction, aversion, delusion, or sometimes by ending their lives.

I know it is a strange concept, but the proof is in the pudding. For example, how many amazing, enlightened men came to their ultimate realization by means of prison? Almost all the Apostles, including Paul, spent months if not years in prison. Sir Thomas Malory spent twenty years in prison writing Le Morte D'Arthur, the first English prose account of the classic legend of King Arthur and the Knights of the Roundtable. Mahatma Gandhi and Nelson Mandela spent years in prison. Even Martin Luther King was arrested more than thirty times and spent a considerable amount of time incarcerated. The list goes on and on.

I am not advocating we break the law simply to serve time in prison or spontaneously join a monastery. Enlightenment is not the result for all who enter the penal system or the cloister. The transformative process that occurs in extremely ascetic conditions is always found in the suck. Whether these conditions are self-imposed or imposed upon us by our Heavenly Father, the circumstances can become fertile soil for transformation and should be savored, not avoided.

As opposed to avoiding suffering, we should dive headfirst into it. As our individual wills are depleted, we consciously surrender ourselves to our Creator. As the will is now united with God's, suffering changes from a source of punishment to a cleansing and purification process. It becomes something we aspire to, not avoid. As this process evolves, we empty ourselves of our attachment to the five senses and earthly things. We sit with the emptiness, stillness, and the infinite nowness of creation and slowly melt the ice that has hardened our hearts. Gradually, through daily practice and conscious surrender of our wills, we return to our Creator and rise again in His name— this time with a burning, full heart, capable of immense, uncon- ditional love and the Passion of Christ.

CHAPTER NINE

THE WARRIOR BODY

*"Do you not know that your body is a temple of
the Holy Spirit who is in you, whom you have
received from God? You are not your own..."*
(1 Corinthians 6:19)

Orthopedic and medical considerations of physical training
"Injuries are the best teachers."
—Stewart Breeding

T he sketch by Leonardo De Vinci entitled "Vitruvian Man"
was drafted in 1490. I share Davinci's fascination with the
human anatomy and can spend hours staring at his illustration.
Close attention should be paid to the drawing, and I recommend
everyone take the opportunity to reflect on it. Notice how the
limbs are outstretched in super-imposed positions creating a
circle and square. If you look closely enough, you can see the
geometric shape of triangles created as the body expands and
contracts. Coincidentally (or maybe not), the circle, square, and
triangle are rudimentary in the mystical teachings of Shinto

and Buddhism. They are known as the "three eternal origins" or Mind, Body, and Spirit.

Notice the magnitude and complexity of the human form and the magnificence manifested in the intelligent design of the most complex creature in the universe. Davinci's drawing attempts to encapsulate the awesomeness of God's greatest creation and how the human body is a physical representation of the entire cosmos.

I have been a trainer, fitness specialist, and strength coach for most of my life. I have had to learn to adjust my methods to orthopedic and medical considerations prior to assigning a fitness regimen. Over the last fifteen years, I have seen a dramatic decline in the overall health of my clients due to obesity and a lifestyle of sitting. We sit to stare at our computers and phones. We sit at work all day, and we sit when we come home. As Americans, we have a new pandemic sweeping the country. Sitting is the new smoking.

Prolonged periods of time spent sitting without proper muscular tension throughout the spine and hips causes the head to protrude forward (especially when staring at a computer) and the upper musculature of the body (T-spine) to collapse. When the T-spine collapses, increased tension is placed on the lumbar or lower spine, adding pressure on the organs and lungs and limiting air capacity.

When we add obesity to the problem of sitting, the core musculature stops firing. Basically, the muscles connecting the hips to the spine stop functioning altogether. When we add gravity to the equation and begin to stand, walk, or run, the entire structure of the body is affected and, if prolonged activity ensues, injury is sure to follow.

The first thing I work on with my clients is postural anatomical adaptation, which is activation of the core musculature, T-spine strength through retraction of shoulder blades while opening the chest, and increasing stability strength throughout the hips, knees, and ankles. I show them a picture of Vitruvian Man and share my thoughts on posture, the cornerstone of Holistic Performance.

Saotome Sensei said the spine is the spiritual antenna. Davinci obviously thought this as well, given the uprightness of Vitruvian Man. In his sketch, the depiction is that of an upright, confident man—not a slouching, broken one. Experimenting with anatomical positions will prove my point.

Stand, but slouch as much as possible. Stick your head forward, collapse your shoulders forward and down, disengage your abdominals, turn your knees in, and just hang out for a second. This posture is the result of chronic sitting. Ask yourself the following questions:

- What is my emotional capacity in this posture?

- What are my mental and physical abilities in this posture?

- Am I confident or scared? Capable or incapable?

Now stand straight up like Vitruvian Man. Arms outstretched, palms facing forward, and ask yourself the same questions. Don't you agree that the difference in the two postures is amazing? How much energy is being leaked throughout the day based on how you stand, sit, or exercise? In addition, continued poor posture may result in injuries or permanent disabilities. Consider daily how you may be standing, sitting, or exercising and continually re-adjust.

Human beings did not evolve over millions of years to stand upright. We were designed that way. Unlike our primate cousins who can walk on two feet, they cannot stand upright due to a lack of muscular development and design, specifically in their gluteus maximus, Medius and piriformis. Primates, with their elongated, powerful arms and hands, were designed for climbing, not walking upright for protracted periods of time.

The glute muscles in human beings and arms that don't drag the ground are largely responsible for our upright posture and bi-pedal locomotion. These same muscles become incredibly weak and will atrophy through prolonged hours of sitting. Therefore, sitting creates a catastrophic, systemic syndrome with emotional, physical, mental, and spiritual effects on human performance, making us more apelike, than manlike.

Science has proven that power positions, like standing upright, shoulders back, chest up, increase testosterone levels, work capacity, and decrease stress levels.

Restoration of your posture and neuro-muscular development of the core musculature and posterior chain is the most critical element when starting and maintaining a fitness regimen and strength training. Without it, you will be ineffective at power distribution. Your stability and balance will be adversely affected, creating new and different movement patterns that lead to injury. Take the time at any point in your training to properly conduct a Functional Movement Screening with a professional, so they may diagnose faulty movement patterns and design an effective corrective exercise program to address these issues.

"Perfect Practice, Makes Perfect"

"I fear not the man who has practiced 10,000 kicks once,
but I fear the man who has practiced
one kick 10,000 times."
—Bruce Lee

As you begin to train, your primary focus should be on the development of kinesthetic awareness, or where your body is in space. Always begin with the concentrated act of standing. Take Vitruvian Man for example:

- Head should be always neutral.

- T-spine (rhomboids, mid traps, and shoulder blades fully retracted), chest up and open.

- Bracing—A certain amount of air should be trapped between the abdominal wall and the spine during movement. Ribs should be drawn down toward the hips and the abdominal wall flexed tight, especially in weighted exercises. The tightness of the brace can be adjusted to the intensity level of weights being used and exercise performed. Bracing allows the three sections of the spine to stay in extension or in alignment and removes the potential for injury.

- Feet should be screwed into the floor with right foot turning clockwise and left foot turning counterclockwise to engage the glutes. A mental projection of one's weight pressing six inches into the floor to create "groundedness" should be maintained throughout all movement.

This practice of overemphasizing standing at the beginning and end of every single repetition will restore proper movement patterns and reestablish perfect, painless posture. Never take this process for granted or forget to examine yourself during training. Almost every strength movement with a barbell or kettlebell either begins or ends with a standing position. To instill a fundamental practice into our fitness/strength programing, I have created 13 golden rules that are the core elements of the Warrior Body Pillar. As mentioned earlier, the other four Pillars are Warrior Mind, Warrior Heart, Warrior Spirit, and Warrior Skillset. Together, they form the practice of holistic performance.

1. Movement

- Practice standing with one-hundred percent concentrated effort. The chances of injury will be greatly diminished, and the benefits will bleed into all performance tasks.

- The progression of movement or exercise choices should be in constant flux and depend largely on personal goals and physiological abilities. Exercise choices always begin with the most basic of movements (such as hinging) and progress to more difficult, functional exercises (such as a single-leg contralateral row). Inclusion of all nine basic movement patterns should be maintained throughout every program design.

- Exercise choices must include all three planes of motion: frontal, sagittal, and transverse.

- There are nine movement patterns everyone, especially the tactical athlete, must include at some point in their fitness and strength-training regimen.

- **Standing** (Previously discussed)

- **Walking**—We are born to walk, not run. Walking is the most restorative, functionally integrated exercise we can do. Our hearts pump oxygen-rich blood to all cells of the body seven days a week, twenty-four hours a day. Getting the carbon dioxide, waste-filled blood back to the heart and lungs is the job of the leg muscles. If we are not moving, our blood flow is seriously restricted and filled with toxicity. I try to walk and/or stand at least eight hours per day and that is probably not enough. Walking is not only the best exercise we can actively engage in daily for our bodies, but also important for our minds and souls.

- **Hinging**—Hinging is the act of isolating and flexing the hip complex solely (with a braced spine position). Think of an athletic position we see in all sports, such as a linebacker in football or how a baseball player stands when waiting for a ball to be hit in their direction. Examples of hinging are sled training, Romanian deadlift, bent row, and good morning. These are extremely effective posterior-chain exercises and should be a central component of all strength-training sessions.

- **Squatting**—Apart from walking, squatting is the most important exercise. Squatting is ancient in its history and is seen in primates. It is the active/rest position, also used in giving birth, relieving ourselves, eating, hunting, gathering, and socializing. Most westerners have lost the mobility required to engage in a full squat position and lack the hip and core stability strength to stand back up properly. This is the first exercise I teach and faithfully reinforce personally and professionally. Perfection of the squat, to include increased range of motion and cyclic loads (heavy and light) of the exercise, is critical to the tactical athlete. Examples and progression of squats are bodyweight squat, goblet squat, front squat (barbell), low bar back squat (barbell).

- **Lunging**—Lunging is a necessary exercise due to its functional nature. The squat takes place in an axial load, meaning the weight of the body and load is split in half then dispersed equally through both feet. While the squat restores primordial movement patterns, the human body does not move in this fashion. We walk or run on one foot and then the other. As the foot strikes the ground, energy is received through the body and moves up through the knee, into the hip, and across the core musculature to the opposite side. This causes the arm to swing forward (anterior and posterior oblique sling). This contralateral motion is the root source of locomotion for the body and therefore must be practiced considerably. The progression for lunging should be stationary first, followed by lunging forward, backward, laterally, and then, if stability allows, single-leg lunging exercises. Lunging exercises include bodyweight, goblet, dumbbells, barbells in front, high or low bar positions, sled training.

- **Pushing**—The act of pushing and pulling with either the upper or lower torso is a comprehensive movement and includes considerable neuromuscular facilitation, large muscle groups, and coordination of the practitioner. For these reasons, it is clear to see how the inclusion of pushing/pulling exercises is extremely beneficial in terms of both efficiency of time and maximal effectiveness of exercise choices. Pushing exercises include sled training, pushups, bench press variations, overhead press, chest press with dumbbells or cable, squats, Olympic lift variations, and leg press variations.

- **Pulling**—Exercises include pullups, pulldowns with cable, row variations, deadlift variations, Olympic lift variations, sled training, rope pulls.

- **Throwing**—The act of throwing ensures athletic development from a concentrated focus on the transverse plain. This range of motion is often neglected in strength training and is critical in weaponizing strength and increasing athleticism. Throwing exercises include landmine variations, sandbag or med-ball throws and slams, chops with cables, bands or bells.

- **Carrying**—Our upper and lower torsos do not link up unless we carry heavy objects. The functionality and comprehensive benefits of carrying heavy objects include increased hypertrophy (muscle size), functional strength, lumbopelvic hip, shoulder, knee, and ankle stability. Carrying heavy objects increases grip strength critical to all Warrior skillset development. Examples of carrying exercises include sled training, farmer carries with barbell, dumbbell, kettlebell, or specifically designed strongman equipment such as a yoke.

NOTE: Pay special attention that sled training is offered as an exercise for all previously mentioned movement patterns, except for throwing and squatting. Sled training, or the "travois," is the original resistance-training method for primitive man. The travois simple design was composed of two long poles with a hide or hides of animals strung between them. This allowed ancient peoples the ability to load the travois with random necessities (including people) that were too heavy and awkward to carry by hand. The travois was a portable device that could also double in functionality as a shelter (lean-to).

In 2009, Army Special Operations Command created a complete tactical-fitness program for its soldiers.[19] The primary function of Tactical Human Optimization Rapid Rehabilitation and Reconditioning (THOR3) was to return wounded or injured soldiers to the fight as quickly as possible. During that time, I worked with several trainers in the THOR3 program who centered the majority of their rehabilitation efforts on sled training with mind-blowing results.

For a solider to be ready for battle again, he must become stronger and be able to carry massive loads over extreme distances. Barbell training and even kettlebell training are unsuitable methods of strength training for progressed injury to the spine, hip, and knees. Sled training, however, allows the practitioner the ability to strengthen the entire kinetic chain just

---

[19] https://www.ncbi.nlm.nih.gov/pmc/articles/PMC4945173/

by walking and with minimal load directly on the joints. It is unusual in that, while offering this strengthening opportunity, the sled doesn't axially load (applying a force on a structure directly along an axis of the structure) the joints with potentially dangerous levels of sheer forces that could further damage the joints. Sled training can be progressive, objective, and performed multiple times a day. It can also be used to train the anterior, posterior kinetic chain, as well as contralateral movement patterns (transverse plane—anterior/posterior oblique sling), which are crucial to athletic development.

Again, sled training is the most advantageous strength training exercise for recovery, longevity, resiliency to injury, and athletic development, bar none!

2. Ten-point fitness training—Over the years, a large part of my career has been dedicated to research and the complexities of programing for our special operations groups and elite law enforcement. The tactical athlete must be good at everything, not great, but good. He must be a generalist in fitness with a broad base of training, endless work capacity, and mental/physical resiliency. Therefore, a comprehensive system and subsequent programing is a prerequisite for anyone considering the Warrior path. This includes civilian sentinels, military, and law enforcement. From this point forward, consider yourself a Tactical Athlete and your fitness regimen must include:

General Fitness Development:

- Strength

- Muscle Endurance

- Body Composition

- Cardio-Vascular endurance

- Flexibility

Performance variables:

- Speed

- Reaction time

- Balance

- Power

- Agility

There are ten dimensions to fitness. Strength is only one. There is no doubt that strength is the most important fitness modality, not only for the tactical athlete but the general fitness enthusiast as well. Strength is the only category of fitness that improves all other nine variables. Strength makes all work easier and leverages the constant increase in work capacity required by the tactical athlete. Since 9/11, strength training has become more popular with Special Operations and is now being instituted as a fundamental component for the training of the regular Army.

Due to an increase in popularity amongst the troops and a serious need to strengthen soldiers readying for deployment and rehabilitate the ones returning, the military has sought out the help of popular strength coaches and organizations, such as the National Strength and Conditioning Association (NSCA). The NSCA's CSCS (certified strength and conditioning specialist) has been the gold-standard certification amongst collegiate strength coaches for the last twenty years. The NSCA has also started a Tactical Strength and Conditioning conference to conduct annual education conferences for coaches and trainers alongside scientific research. As of this writing, the military affiliates itself with NSCA guidelines in programing for special operations, as well as regular infantry units. The military also requires strength coaches and fitness specialists to be CSCS certified.

The drawback is that the NSCA's background is largely based in programing for collegiate athletes, especially football. We have all seen the highlights on ESPN with the University of Alabama or Clemson's strength coach barking and screaming in the background at dozens of young aspiring players doing squats, presses, and cleans for three to five reps followed by five-minute rest breaks.

College strength coaches have the benefit of preparing for the season during the summer months. They utilize periodization programming, which is a means of systematic, progressive overload, to increase the strength level and muscle size of their athletes. They also have the advantage of knowing approximately how long a game will last. They know the location, the forecasted weather, how long their athletes will be on the field, and how long they can rest before the next game.

None of this is relevant to the tactical athlete. Training a tactical athlete using periodized methodologies of any kind, such as linear, undulating, or block designs, will fall flat on its face. Training a tactical athlete using basic, sagittal-plane compound exercises, such as squats, deadlifts, and presses primarily with barbells in axial-loaded positions, will increase maximal strength but also exacerbate muscular instabilities.

The objective increase in strength pertaining to pounds lifted will not translate to the battlefield, which is kinetic, chaotic, and occurs in all three planes of motion at one time.

I'm not saying we shouldn't use barbells or incorporate these compound lifts into our programming, we should. But they should only be roughly thirty to forty percent of the totality of programming required by the tactical athlete. The absolute most critical element to the tactical athlete is a "Mindbody" approach to training which is NOT currently mass produced nor even considered by the NSCA or any other strength training organizations.

3. Mindbody/Mind Muscle Connection

The Mindbody or "Mind Muscle" connection is the most important modality to fitness and strength development. This is the single greatest resource for consciously achieving the flow state. During physical training, we can multiply the physical benefits of exercise and practice the holistic inclusion of the mental, emotional, and spiritual energies. This is accomplished by following the same protocol we will discuss in the upcoming chapter, "The Warrior Spirit," regarding the practice of meditation. I refer to this as "Meditraining." Its basic components are:

- **Mindfulness** of breath and the tactical manipulation of exhaling, inhaling, and bracing consciously to maximize the effects of the exercise, decrease stress, and increase recovery time.

- **Attention** on the spine and posture during exercise.

- **Awareness** of internal cues, such as where our bodies are in space, thoughts, feelings, or stress, and appropriate self-talk strategies. In addition, awareness of external cues from a coach, sounds, distractions, and self-talk strategies. All must be addressed as they arise.

- Complete and total **focus** on the task at hand. All effort should be made to hyper-focus on the exercise, the movement, the muscle, the breath — all happening right here, right now. No consideration should be paid to clocks, repetitions, sets, or time spent in the gym. We have objective data technologies and clocks to do this for us. Do not allow the monkey mind to manifest itself during training, especially during high levels of suck.

Pour yourself into the process of Meditraining with each session. You should be exhausted physically and mentally from the sheer effort of maintaining your focused intent. As we advance our practice of Meditraining, a natural tendency to fall into a state of flow will almost always occur. I have performed countless strength and fitness tests on clients during the flow phenomena, and I am always blown away. Much of our energy during training is bled out by our minds and the constant negative self-talk offered by our egos. Meditraining prevents this from happening. The flow experience increases the potential for superhuman capacities and aligns all four energies (mental, emotional, physical, and spiritual) that we do not have access to in dual states of consciousness.

4. Accommodating Resistance

I am one to give credit where credit is due. Louie Simmons is arguably the greatest strength coach ever. He owns and operates Westside Barbell in Columbus, Ohio, and has over 140 world records to his name. Over the years, Simmons has developed his own strength-training philosophies and influenced the strength community through countless inventions and methodologies.

I think Louie's greatest contribution is the use of accommodating resistance, the process of using bands or chains in addition to a barbell or weighted device. This allows the strength curve to be reversed, a full contraction of the muscle throughout the entire range of motion, and development of speed and power through the end range of the exercise. For example, if you were to place 50 pounds of bands over a two-hundred-pound weighted bar and perform a low-bar back squat, the bar would be 250 pounds at the top (end range) of the exercise and 200 pounds at the bottom. This allows progressive overload and time under tension of the lifter without the weight altering the mechanics at the bottom of the exercise, which is always the most difficult.

The lifter can experience the full range of motion with decreased load at the bottom, the most precarious moment of the exercise, and then explode into a standing position. This builds speed strength, power, and weaponizes the standing position. It also forces the glutes and posterior chain to contract more intensely and stand up with a heavier load.

I use bands and chains everywhere possible in my training. The continued use of accommodating strength will not only increase maximal speed, stability, and general strength capacities, but it will prolong the lifter's career, minimize injury, and kill many a bird with one stone.

5. Professional Coaching

There's no way around it. If you want to excel at fitness/ strength training (or any skill for that matter), hiring a professional can save you massive amounts of time, frustration, and possibly career-ending injuries. I won't spend much time on this subject because it speaks for itself. I completely understand the financial constraints regarding working with an expert worthy of your time. However, if you find the right coach, the money you spend will be paid back threefold in terms of progress, education, and consistency, which is where goals become reality. If you are serious about strength training and learning the intricacies of kettlebell or the power/Olympic lifts, you must hire a solid coach.

6. Hormones and Recovery

Our physical bodies are completely reliant on healthy hormone production. For men that means testosterone. Without adequate levels of testosterone, it is virtually impossible to lose body fat, build muscle, or recover from tough workouts. Before beginning a fitness/strength regimen, I recommend all my male clients see a hormone specialist to assess current testosterone levels and possible solutions for hormone therapy.

There are dozens of over-the-counter testosterone enhancement ergogenics available on the market. It is quite possible that a natural solution will work for you, but this should be a conversation between you and your physician. Proper nutrition and sleep are critical to maintaining proper levels of testosterone and help decrease potentially harmful hormones like cortisol.

7. Nutrition

Today there are more diet trends than there are types of food and discussing them would require another chapter, probably confusing you further. Everyone needs all three macronutrients in a well-balanced, clean diet, especially if you are fueling performance. This includes carbohydrates. No two people are remotely the same, and nowhere is this truer than with nutrition programing. Without proper fueling, workouts are almost pointless. I highly recommend a macro-based nutrition program. The problem with a macro approach is that there can be quite a learning curve required on your part, and it is quite expensive to have a professional do it for you. Until then, let me share with you what I call the **Survivor Diet**.

A. Throughout the week (6 days) eat only fresh, whole foods you would find in the wild.

    •   Red meat, poultry, fish, eggs

    •   Berries, seasonal fruits, and Vegetables

    •   Nuts

    •   Tubers

    •   Grains, such as steel cut oats, quinoa, brown rice

B. Eat three meals per day, cooking and prepping each meal. Try to place your meals six hours apart. If your workload is high, add two snacks three hours after breakfast and after lunch. This will keep your body's glucose levels balanced and prevent bonking. It will also keep you in a high level of fat metabolism, if your workload is consistent.

C. The seventh day of each week is cheat day. Pretend you have made it out of the woods and stumbled on a Dairy Queen. Eat whatever you like (within reason), and chances are you will not be too fond of fast food or alcohol after a week of clean eating.

Fasting: Significant research has been conducted over the last ten years about fasting and its effects on performance. Fasting can indeed be beneficial to your overall physical and spiritual health to include:

- Healthier body composition

- Detox of organs and tissue

- Reduction of insulin resistance

- Lowering inflammation

- Improving blood pressure and cholesterol levels

- Increasing growth hormone

- Delaying aging and degeneration

Fasting can be intermittent with a four- to five-hour eating window, or periodically with the inclusion of a three- to seven-day fast, ingesting only water or adding juices and broth.

Never forget, your true self is the face of God. He is always there, but layers of muck and filth cover the mirror and block His reflection. Fasting, eating clean, and removing toxins out of the blood stream and brain are not meant to be punishment. There is a much greater experience waiting for us on the other side — greater than any day of couch-riding with a twelve-pack, a bag of Fritos, and Netflix. Living clean is like riding a bike. It's going to take a while to get your balance. Stay objective. Stay honest. Stay the course.

8. Supplementation & Recovery

Supplementation can be confusing. For me, supplementation is just that, supplementation. I only supplement what I feel my body isn't getting from proper nutrition. I take vitamins D, C, and B12, Quercetin, zinc, echinacea, and fish oil every day. These maximize my immune system and add an extra layer of protection. It's important that you check with your physician about appropriate levels of each vitamin. If my daily protein intake is low, I supplement with protein powders or bars. I recommend approximately one gram of protein per pound, if you are actively performing a basic strength-training program. For an activity level that is high or the volume from strength training is considerable, increase this to 1.5 grams.

Creatine is another commonly used and scientifically verified supplement that can aid in hypertrophy (increased muscle size), recovery, and even strength gain.

Remember K.I.S.S.: "Keep it simple, stupid," when it comes to hormone therapy, nutrition, recovery, and supplementation. An optimal testosterone level is critical for performance-based training and cognitive function, emotional stability, and energy. Do not forego an objective assessment of T-levels and the therapies required to maintain them. Once this box has been checked, keep your immune system cranking with the cocktail I mentioned above.

If a nutrition program is working for you, stick with it. Dump a short-term program in favor of something you like and can maintain for the rest of your life. Sleep as much as possible. When needed, take advantage of massages and healing therapies, such as hot and cold treatments. Just like fitness, progress with nutrition and recovery strategies is about consistency, discipline, and effort—not short-term fixes!

9. Objective Volume vs Subjective Volume

Fitness is predicated on the overall summation, or additive effects, of training over a certain amount of time. Summation is calculated by the amount of volume an athlete accrues over a training cycle. Volume is the total of every rep, set, exercise, and bouts of exercise per week, month, and year. All fitness and strength progressions are based on volume. Not enough volume, no need for physiological adaptations. Too much volume and the system will collapse from mental, neurological, and physical fatigue, often with accompanying injury. This is especially true for first-time exercisers, folks with orthopedic or medical considerations, and age-related restrictions.

Objective volume is simply a mathematical calculation, a multiplication problem. For example, say you completed five sets of bench press at two hundred pounds per set for five reps or, as written by a strength coach, 5x5x200. The total volume for that bout of exercise would be 5,000 pounds of volume. Tracking objective volume is the central ingredient for programing and a practical approach for increasing intensity levels. We must include objective volume tracking in our fitness/ strength regimen. However, we should not become addicted to this process nor think we are now a math problem rather than a human being subject to disturbances in training. These disturbances could be illness, injury, fatigue, work, stress, wrong exercise choices, or mistakes in programing. For this reason, a more accurate means of programing is combining objective tracking alongside subjective volume, or the use of RPE— Rating of Perceived Exertion.

RPE is how a weight feels given a certain rep range or how intense a bout of exercise may seem, subjectively. RPE allows us to adjust our objective programing in real time to either increase or decrease volume, given the subjective experience of the exerciser. A good way to begin using RPE is to grade an exercise set or rep on a scale of one to ten, in terms of work expenditure or how heavy a weight feels while using.

For example, if you do a set of bench presses for five reps with 200 pounds and you could have done seven reps with that same weight, the RPE would be roughly an eight out of ten. If you did five reps with 200 pounds and could not do six reps, the weight would be a ten RPE. A strength coach might want to leave some room in the tank and write a workout like this: 5x5x7 RPE. Instead of saying 5x5x200 pounds, using a 7 RPE gives the lifter the opportunity to increase the weight if the weight feels light that day and decrease the weight if the weight feels heavy.

10. Integrating Objective Technologies with Ratings of Perceived Exertion

The advances in objective technologies to aid in fitness programing and recovery are astonishing and continue to be updated almost daily. There are apps or wearables for almost everything fitness-related. I don't suggest investing thousands of dollars on gear you likely do not need and probably cannot figure out how to use, but here are a couple of suggestions for how to apply objective data to your programing for greater results.

- Use body composition analysis, such as Inbody or BodPod, as opposed to scales that only show total body weight, not composition. We do not care about body-weight. We care how much muscle and how much fat you have in terms of pounds. There is absolutely no reason for a man to be more than 13 percent bodyfat.

- Apps that calculate objective volume and produce spreadsheets for more effective programing.

- Wearables that track recovery, such as the Oura™ ring or the Whoop™.

- Video analysis of movement patterns during exercise for evaluation by a coach and corrective exercise strategies.

- Heart-rate trackers

I have spent considerable time over the last decade combining heart-rate training technologies with my clients' subjective perceived ranges of exertion (see my second book, *The BioHacker*). The benefits of objective data (for example, current heart rate during exercise) combined with real-time RPE levels experienced by my clients is priceless. Most people do not have a good understanding of their potential exertion levels or how hard they can push themselves when they begin training. Many either quit before reaching effective exertion levels or continue to train at inappropriately high heart-rate levels for prolonged periods of time. The latter leads to injury or overtraining.

Performing an objective VO_2 test or a subjective rating of perceived exertion test using a bike or treadmill can help to determine *individualized max heart rate and training zone.* Once you have established your individual training zones, this can be paired with *individualized RPE,* which reinforces accurate perceptions of the clients HR and intensity levels. This allows the exerciser to work without objective technologies and still accurately record heart rate (HR) if necessary. It will also show fluctuations in HR. As the HR goes down over time, as the exerciser's cardiovascular system accommodates to training, it will go back up if the exerciser down-trains.

11. The Amish WOD (Workout Design)

I highly respect my Amish and Mennonite brothers and sisters and their way of life. They do a lot of things right, and we should all figure out how to sell our stuff and move to the farm. I call this workout design the Amish WOD because it is so hard, requires massive work capacity, makes you stronger, and promises to put a slab of dense muscle on your frame without spending countless hours in the gym.

The Amish WOD is a circuit. Without getting into the science of it, a circuit is the best way to increase the ten dimensions of fitness, general physical preparedness (GPP), all nine movement patterns and, again, build massive work capacity. The Amish WOD does require some gear, but you can add to your garage gym as needed and make do in the meantime. It is a combination of five to six exercises with at least three compound lifts, all three planes of motion, all nine movement patterns, and at least one maximal lift performed in a circuit. The exercises are in repetitions, not time, with as much rest needed between sets so as to complete the next exercise with maximal effort (think farm work) and done for a total of anywhere between 40-60 full circuits. Total time lasts from one to two hours to be performed one to three times per week. The WOD looks something like this:

- Exercise #1: Deadlift with bands—maximal strength, posterior chain, speed strength, whole body, sagittal plane, standing, hinging, pulling

- Exercise #2: Chops with sandbag—whole body, core-centric, transverse plane, hinging, squatting, throwing, carrying

- Exercise #3: Kettlebell Turkish getups—whole body, all three planes of motion, extremely functional, hinging, lunging, pushing, carrying

- Exercise #4: Split Jerk (barbell)—Whole body, power production, stability strength, frontal and sagittal plane

- Exercise #5: Navy seals with band—whole body, core-centric, frontal and transverse plane, pushing, standing, hinging, squatting

- Exercise #6: Single-leg Bent row (landmine barbell)— posterior chain, contralateral, all three planes of motion, standing, hinging, lunging, pulling

12. Entering the Suck

There is no way around it. For the tactical athlete, time spent in the suck is a prerequisite. I often say, "Strength wins battles. Endurance and stamina allow you to get up the next day and do it all over again." Tactical athletes must utilize fitness training as a means of attaining holistic energy integration. It must also become a means of stress inoculation.

The tactical athlete should integrate moments in which absolute failure and anerobic (without oxygen) threshold are not only reached but maintained. As lactic acid is being dumped into the muscle, neural drive and conscious control of the body begins to break down. The mind begins to slip into the "black" where negative self-talk and quitting become overwhelming options. This is a prime training opportunity to keep the Meditraining process, and focus all your conscious intent on the experience at hand.

Stay objective during this process. Remove yourself by *watching* your mind and body fail, as opposed to being the *victim* of it. Training in the suck is essential to increasing your tolerance levels of lactic acid, psychological impacts of being in the black, and the physiological impediments which follow.

Do *not* spend too much time in the suck, or overtraining will occur and cessation of exercise will follow. Learning how to implement brief moments of suck into weekly sessions, utilizing smart exercise choices and incorporating the RPE scale, is one of the greatest tools a Warrior can have.

Train smarter and harder over time. Learn to listen to the wisdom of your body. It often knows better than your fancy heart-rate tracker or any app you download. Stick to the exercises you can perform with perfect range of motion and postural integrity. *Never* progress into a movement or a weight in which you fail for a single repetition. Practice does not make perfect; perfect practice makes perfect. Never forget progress in strength and fitness training is reliant on all the boring words most folks dislike, such as discipline, dedication, internal fortitude, humility, and drive.

Slow is smooth and smooth is fast. Each session in the gym should be a learning experience through which the warrior continues to learn about the depth of his spirit, heart, and body. Never dismiss or disrespect this process. The gym is a *dojo*, or training hall, where we look at ourselves in the mirror and continue studying and perfecting technique.

Stay objective when ego and moments of your false self show up for a training session. Don't judge yourself too harshly. Leave room for improvement and remember that your body, just like the universe, is in constant flux.

For more advanced training strategies, please consider my book, *Biohacker,* or these texts: *Supertraining* by Mel Siff; Serious *Strength Training* by Tudor Bampa; *Special Strength Development for All Sports* by Louie Simmons.

13. Scheduling

One of the simplest and most effective means of transformation is scheduling your most valuable commodity—time. Be honest with your time, especially if you have a family. Family always comes first, but you can find clever ways to include your wife or children into your training schedule. Make no exceptions or excuses. Prepare your schedule for the week on Sunday and do your best to adhere to your calendar.

I won't say it's easy to fit everything in; it's not. My 52-year-old body is constantly sore, and every minute of every day is accounted for. Welcome to the world of Warrior training! But remember, nothing worth having ever comes easily.

CHAPTER TEN

THE WARRIOR SKILLSET

*"It's better to be a warrior in a garden
than a gardener in a war."*
— *Ancient Samurai Proverb*

Are you familiar with the Bill of Rights, as written by our country's Founding Fathers? These first ten amendments to the United States Constitution spell out our rights and freedoms in relation to our government. Every American Warrior — in fact, every American citizen — should be thoroughly familiar with these amendments, written to help preserve and protect an entirely new form of government. They are:

Amendment 1—Freedom of Religion, Speech, and the Press

Congress shall make no law respecting an establishment of religion or prohibiting the free exercise thereof or abridging the freedom of speech or of the press, or the right of the people peaceably to assemble and to petition the government for a redress of grievances.

Amendment 2 — The Right to Bear Arms

A well-regulated Militia being necessary to the security of a free State, the right of the people to keep and bear Arms shall not be infringed.

Amendment 3 — The Housing of Soldiers

No soldier shall, in time of peace, be quartered in any house without the consent of the owner, nor in time of war but in a manner to be prescribed by law.

Amendment 4 — Protection from Unreasonable Searches and Seizures

The right of the people to be secure in their persons; houses, papers, and effects against unreasonable searches and seizures shall not be violated, and no warrants shall issue but upon probable cause, supported by oath or affirmation, and particularly describing the place to be searched and the persons or things to be seized.

Amendment 5 — Protection of Rights to Life, Liberty, and Property

No person shall be held to answer for a capital or otherwise infamous crime unless on a presentment or indictment of a grand jury, except in cases arising in the land or naval forces, or in the militia, when in actual service in time of war or public danger; nor shall any person be subject for the same offense to be twice put in jeopardy of life or limb; nor shall be compelled in any criminal case to be a witness against himself, nor be deprived of life, liberty, or property without due process of law; nor shall private property be taken for public use without just compensation.

Amendment 6—Rights of Accused Persons in Criminal Cases

In all criminal prosecutions, the accused shall enjoy the right to a speedy and public trial by an impartial jury of the state and district wherein the crime shall have been committed, which district shall have been previously ascertained by law, and to be informed of the nature and cause of the accusation; to be confronted with the witnesses against him; to have compulsory process for obtaining witnesses in his favor; and to have the assistance of counsel for his defense.

Amendment 7—Rights in Civil Cases

In suits at common law, where the value in controversy shall exceed twenty dollars, the right of trial by jury shall be preserved, and no fact tried by a jury shall be otherwise reexamined in any court of the United States than according to the rules of the common law.

Amendment 8—Excessive Bail, Fines, and Punishments Forbidden

Excessive bail shall not be required, nor excessive fines imposed, nor cruel and unusual punishments inflicted.

Amendment 9—Other Rights Kept by the People

The enumeration in the Constitution of certain rights shall not be construed to deny or disparage others retained by the people.

Amendment 10—Undelegated Powers Kept by the States and the People

The powers not delegated to the United States by the Constitution, nor prohibited by it to the states, are reserved to the states respectively, or to the people.

"Give me liberty or give me death." *—Patrick Henry*

Apart from the Holy Bible, I believe the words penned in the Declaration of Independence and the Constitution of the United States of America by our Founding Fathers are the most divinely inspired documents in existence.

If followed as written, the absolute brilliance of our separate, three-tiered Federal government system—Judicial, Legislative and Executive branches—makes it virtually impossible for any individual branch to exceed its powers, as granted by the peoples and clearly defined in the Constitution.

Despite common terminology frequently used to describe our country's government, we are *not* a democracy. Careful consideration was paid by our Founding Fathers to deny a populace majority, which is a democracy, the ability to overwhelm a minority whose voice would otherwise be stifled by such a system.

So that all peoples would have an equal voice and vote, our Founding Fathers created a Constitutional Republic. This Republic recognized an electoral system that evened out large populaces of citizens located in cities and towns with less populated rural areas and states. This form of government also placed the majority of power with the individual states, local municipalities, and elected officials who serve the wishes of their constituents, not within the Federal government.

At the cornerstone of our rule of law, as drafted in the Declaration of Independence and then ten years later in the Constitution, lies the most enlightened, spiritually inspired passage ever drafted as the basis for a newly developed nation and its free peoples.

"We hold these truths to be self-evident, that all men are created equal, that they are endowed by their Creator with certain unalienable Rights, that among these are Life, Liberty and the pursuit of Happiness..."

It may seem ridiculous to many who do not know our history, but, before our Founding Fathers put pen to paper, this concept of unalienable rights never existed. The United States was a colony of Great Britain and a possession of its king. The monarchy was the entire government, and it owned all property, monies, commodities, and peoples under its rule. In the history of the world, never had a document been drafted forming a nation of free peoples whose rights of life, liberty, property, and the pursuit of happiness were granted to them by the Almighty, and, therefore, cannot be appointed or stripped away by any government, foreign or domestic.

Our forefathers intuitively drew from their combined experiences with tyrannical governments and monarchies to form the Bill of Rights detailing each citizens' civil liberties and the core of our rule of law. They knew their hope for a free republic would not survive its infancy without the thoughtful consideration of the Second Amendment. It is my belief, based on many of our Founding Fathers' deep convictions as Christians and followers of Jesus Christ, that they knew the moment these immortal words came into existence, the newly born republic would be under constant attack by the forces of evil.

From the moment the Declaration of Independence was signed, our country has been under a constant, massive spiritual attack. As of today, that attack has never been so transparent— not just by the barbarian horde at the gate, but from within.

An Army of One

"Out of every one hundred men, ten shouldn't even be there. Eighty are just targets. Nine are the real fighters. And we are lucky to have them, for they make the battle. Ah, but the one, one is the warrior, and he will bring the others back."
—Spartan Warrior Adage

It is one thing to be granted the tremendous responsibility to keep and bear arms; it is yet another to accept the inherent responsibility of becoming highly capable of manipulating those arms proficiently. To be clear, the Second Amendment states: *"A well-regulated Militia, being necessary to the security of a free State, the right of the people to keep and bear Arms, shall not be infringed."* I am obviously not a constitutional scholar, but the Second Amendment clearly outlines the intentions of the Founders.

Not only is it abundantly clear that the right to keep and bear arms *shall not be infringed,* but the Second Amendment also goes a step further: *"A well-regulated Militia, being necessary to the security of a free State"* clearly implies that, as free men, we share the immense responsibility of becoming tactically skilled with those firearms we bear, especially if needed to fight for a common cause.

The Second Amendment was drafted after the Revolution while America still had a Continental Army, but it wasn't under Federal control. Massive debate among the Founders circulated for two years before the standing Federal Army was created on September 29, 1789. Even with the creation of the Federal Army, no attempt was made, nor debate heard, to remove the Second Amendment due to the existence of a standing Army. The Founding Fathers held onto a shared, sincere distrust of government (for good reason) and many, to include Madison and Jefferson, fought tooth and nail to deny our fledgling nation its own standing army for fear it could be turned against its own peoples.

To clarify, from inception, the Founders never intended for power to be held in the centralized halls of the Federal government. The Second Amendment to the Constitution of the United States of America assures that power always stays with the people, for the people, and by the people.

It is *our* responsibility as free men to defend our Republic "from enemies both foreign and domestic," including defense of our civil liberties. Living up to that standard requires extensive education in the art of warfare, not as a means of destruction but as a deterrent to those with evil intentions bent on the demise of God, country, and liberty.

Skillset Development

COMBATIVES

> *"When somebody challenges you, fight back!*
> *Be brutal, be tough."*
> *—Donald Trump*

Walking the Warrior path requires daily practice of our martial skills. Those skills include proficiency with armed (bladed weapons/firearms) and unarmed combatives, such as urban and outdoor survival.

Today there are countless martial arts available to the consumer. With the popularity of MMA, learning the basics of unarmed combat is more convenient than ever before. Every Warrior must learn to proficiently strike with:

- Fingers

- Hands

- Elbows

- Shoulders

- Head

- Hip

- Knees

- Feet

To learn effective striking, the best martial arts are Western boxing, Muay Thai boxing, Tae Kwon Do, and various forms of Karate and Wing Chun.

Everyone should learn the basics of offensive and defensive grappling and ground fighting found in martial arts, such as wrestling, Jiu-Jitsu, Sambo, and Judo. While sporting martial arts are excellent at developing skill and gameness, one must be mindful not to become addicted to the "rules" found in sporting martial arts, and always train in a realistic manner so as not to develop life-threatening habits. Always train as though there are multiple attackers who may possess a bladed weapon, blunt instrument, or firearm. Never let down your guard. Always remain vigilant, and never forget the true enemy is the one within.

The same rules apply to weapons manipulation. Just because you have a gun and a license to carry it doesn't mean you know how to kinetically use it in a defensive or offensive manner. Massive amounts of technology and skillset development of handguns and rifles (long and short range) have accelerated exponentially since the attacks of September 11. The marketplace is filled with former Special Forces operators who are highly skilled and more than willing to offer their services in person or even online.

While it is not recommended, if money becomes an obstacle, there is a massive amount of education and training to be found on social-media platforms and the Internet. Pursuing your training will undoubtedly cost you in terms of dollars and time spent, but, if you are to carry a firearm or plan to defend your home, training and proficiency with that firearm is not an option.

LIVELIHOOD

"Entrepreneurship is about turning what excites you in life
into capital, so that you can do more of it
and move forward with it."
—Richard Branson

Our Constitution, which allows us life, liberty, and pursuit of happiness, implies that we have the ability to manifest that happiness. It is not the responsibility of the government to carry us through life. It is up to us and us alone. If we are not actively pursuing our entrepreneurial dreams, then we are merely existing, not living. We should always be striving to achieve our utmost potential and create better lives for ourselves and loved ones no matter our race, gender, or religious beliefs.

This process, afforded us by our Constitution, is like any other. Small, incremental changes and calculated risks can and will lead to incredible opportunities. Many times, this means starting a side gig. Side gigs offer us two opportunities: 1) the opportunity to start a new business without potential risk and investment; 2) added cash flow, which means redundancy.

Redundancy must become front and center in our planning and execution for everything we do. Redundancy means "one is none, and two is one". For example, I have a great job, but what happens if I get injured or terminated? I have a freezer filled with a six-month supply of meat. That's great, but what happens if the electricity is cut off? I have a basement filled with a six-month supply of canned meats and vegetables. But what do I do when that runs out? I keep my truck topped off with gasoline and a 50-gallon drum filled with extra petrol. But what do I do when that is burned up and gas stations are shut down? I have thousands of rounds of ammunition, firearms, bulletproof armor chest rig, and the ability to use them. But what if they are stolen or destroyed in a fire?

True preparation includes all contingencies in every area of our lives. We need to become true Renaissance men like our Founding Fathers, who spoke multiple languages, understood business and commerce, were master statesmen, writers, speakers, thinkers, expert farmers, and tactically proficient with weaponry and self-defense. We should all take a lesson from these amazing men and constantly educate ourselves on both urban and outdoor survival skills.

Outdoor Survival

- Land navigation

- Fishing and hunting (to include preparation and storage)

- Weather prediction

- First aid

- Primitive weapons and toolmaking

- Primitive shelter assembly

- Snares and traps

- Flora and fauna for possible food and medicine

Urban Survival

- Threat assessment

- How to pack a "go bag"

- Emergency food, fuel, and water

- Weapons and ammunition

- Survival hacks (think MacGyver)

- Storage, clothing, batteries, miscellaneous supplies

- First aid

- Transportation

PART THREE
LIVING THE WARRIOR LIFE

CHAPTER ELEVEN

THE CONCEPT OF "MU JU NO SHIN" OR "NO ABIDING MIND"

"When a person does not think, 'Where shall I put it?' the mind will extend throughout the entire body and move to any place at all... The effort not to stop the mind in just one place—this is discipline. Not stopping the mind is object and essence. Put it nowhere and it will be everywhere. Even in moving the mind outside the body, if it is sent in one direction, it will be lacking in nine others. If the mind is not restricted to just one direction, it will be in all ten. Presumably, as a martial artist, I do not fight for gain or loss, I am not concerned with strength or weakness, and neither advance a step nor retreat a step. The enemy does not see me. I do not see the enemy. Penetrating to a place where heaven and earth have not yet divided, where yin and yang have not yet arrived, I quickly and necessarily gain effect."

T his excerpt taken from *The Unfettered Mind* was written by the 17th-century Zen master Takuan Soho (1573-1645). *The Unfettered Mind* is possibly the greatest book ever written on the art of swordsmanship and the cultivation of right mind and intention. It was intended as a guide for the infamous samurai Warrior, Yagyu Munenori, a great swordsman and rival to the legendary Miyamoto Musashi. Takuan, a giant in the history of Zen, was also a gardener, calligrapher, poet, author, and adviser to samurai and shoguns.

In these pointed essays, Takuan shares his deep understanding of the mind, both generally and its nature when faced with conflict. *The Unfettered Mind* had a massive influence on samurai for generations. It especially affected Japan's most infamous sword fighter Miyamoto Musashi. Musashi would go on to draft, arguably, the most popular book in the world concerning samurai wisdom and mindset, *The Book of Five Rings*.

Every Warrior *must* study the classics of Takuan Soho and Musashi, if for no other reason than to witness the amazing superhuman potential waiting to be unleashed once we face our greatest fear: death. First and foremost, the samurai constantly wrestled with the concept of "losing" or "dropping" the self (ego) and its absolute aversion to death. From his first waking moment until he laid down to sleep, a samurai was required to be ready, willing, and able to sacrifice his life to his master. This blind obedience can best be viewed through the practice of *hara-kiri*, or ritual suicide by disembowelment. Fear of death is obviously a profoundly serious problem for a samurai who may become paralyzed in the heat of battle or is unwilling to take his own life to protect the honor of himself and his master.

The ego is the "false self," or the mask we all develop over time, the "who" we think we are. It is an ongoing psychological phenomenon that weaves from the environment, both internal and external, small pieces of life experience into a blanket we call our "self." The essence of the ego is attachment. The essence of "no self" or "no mind/mu-shin" coincidentally is *non-attachment*. No less than the same non-attachment sought by the ancient saints such as John of the Cross or the Boddhisatva, who ironically lived halfway across the planet about six hundred years before Jesus. I find it absolutely fascinating that a Spanish monk, an Indian prince, and a Japanese samurai, separated by immense time and space, were pursuing the same spiritual resolution. Though their motives were vastly different, they all arrived at the same destination. This divine phenomenon should never be lost on us.

The ego constantly attaches itself to earthly things, beliefs or thoughts, and emotional forms produced by those thoughts. None is more intense than its attachment to life and its weaponization of fear to "stay alive." The ego's attachment to thought form is like nitrous oxide for the "*mind*." The perpetual hamster wheel of unconscious thought production. The ego fused with the unconscious mind is in and of itself the opposite of *Christ consciousness,* which is the pinnacle of Warriordom and the sole intent of this book.

When unconscious mind and ego become inseparable, with no objective space between them, we become victimized by those thoughts, the emotions, and the action or inaction that follows. The ego's delusion and iron grip with which it clamps onto life can, during inopportune moments, fuel a paralyzing phobia of death. Lt. Colonel Dan Grossman refers to this state as the "black." This phobia also happens to be of utmost concern to samurai Warriors who routinely stare death squarely in the face and obviously cannot afford a moment's hesitation during a sword fight.

On Killing and *On Combat* investigate the physiological and psychological effects combat places on the entirety of the human organism. The "black" is the state of mind that takes place when the ego finds itself in a life-threatening situation, and stimulus from the exterior universe becomes assimilated into the mind. The ego dominates the consciousness and central nervous system and impedes the Warrior's ability to form rational analysis and subsequent action in a given situation. It is akin to putting molasses in a Lamborghini. You are going nowhere, fast.

Another term used for this mental state is "paralysis by analysis." When you reach *Condition Black*, your heart is instantly at its maximum rate. At this level of arousal, even a well-trained Warrior will experience catastrophic breakdown of both mental and physical performance. The physiological symptoms that accompany the black are tunnel vision, auditory exclusion, deterioration of complex motor skills, and bladder and bowel evacuation.

In high-stress, life-or-death situations, sphincter and bladder control are not a priority for the human organism. During these situations, deep-rooted, ancient survival tactics override the central nervous system. Our body subsequently will excrete all waste products in a heated attempt to fight or flee, making the organism less attractive to predators. At this point, any cognitive process and accompanying signals to the central nervous system are completely overridden.

In anonymous surveys conducted after World War II, twenty-five percent of soldiers admitted they wet themselves during combat and one-eighth admitted to defecating. Most researchers believe that number to be much higher.

Extreme vasoconstriction is also typically present in Condition Black. Vasoconstriction is when the blood vessels narrow to constrict blood flow. In life-or-death situations, your body wants most of your blood to stay near vital organs and large muscles that can be used to fight or flee. One potential benefit is that vasoconstriction helps limit the amount of bleeding you experience if you were to sustain a wound. Extreme vasoconstriction causes people to look white with fear, as all the blood has been shunted away from the skin's surface to more vital parts of the body. While vasoconstriction serves as a handy survival mechanism, its progression unfortunately leads to deterioration of complex motor skills, such as firing a weapon or ducking under a sword.

During Condition Black, the more evolved forebrain shuts down and the primitive middle brain and brain stem assume control. Grossman refers to this as the "puppy dog" brain. Without executive functioning, you are subject to incredible levels of irrational thinking such as fighting, freezing, or fleeing. For example, many soldiers during the First and Second World Wars reported observing other soldiers running from behind a defensive position directly into enemy fire for no reason. To quote Grossman, "In Condition Black you can run, and you can fight like a big, hairless, clawless bear, but that is about all you are capable of doing."

If Condition Black is at the far left of the spectrum, the "Flow State" or "Flow Consciousness" is at the far right. Flow exemplifies *non-dual conscious* state. It can be described as a combination of activity, extreme mental focus of all faculties, and a "letting go" of expectations and ramifications (even the possibility of death).

Steven Kotler, author of *The Rise of Superman* and founder of the Human Genome Project, seems to agree saying, "Since flow is a fluid action state, making better decisions isn't enough: we also have to act on those decisions. The problem is fear, which stands between us and all actions. Yet our fears are grounded in self, time, and space. With our sense of self out of the way, we are liberated from doubt and insecurity. With time gone, there is no yesterday to regret or tomorrow to worry about. And when our sense of space disappears, so do physical consequences. But when all three vanish at once, something far more incredible occurs: our fear of death—that most fundamental of all fears—can no longer exist. Simply put: if you are infinite and atemporal, you cannot die."

In *The Rise of Superman*, Kotler interviews dozens of big-wave riders, free climbers, skydivers, and motocross daredevils who have actively pursued the flow state, in order to perform superhuman feats. If we just sit and contemplate the ridiculousness of a big-wave rider who is terrified of getting on top of a 100-foot wave with a six-foot surfboard, we can begin to understand the absolute necessity of this mindset. The problem is that this concept of flow flies in the face of current thoughts on the subject offered by many clinicians and researchers whom I have interviewed. These scholars, coincidentally, have never personally experienced the flow state during death-defying activity.

Their position is that flow only occurs unconsciously, meaning we have no ability to manipulate or induce this state of consciousness, and we can only experience flow with the right amount of stress. If the stress is too low, no flow. Too high, no flow. What I believe they fail to comprehend is that the flow state is being replicated by these superhuman daredevils every day, and they are actively experiencing the flow state during death-defying activity. I personally can attest to flow consciousness occurring while in life-threatening situations.

In my estimation, the experts got this one wrong. History clearly demonstrates the ancient samurai recognized the flow state centuries ago and then set forth on a mission to systematize and weaponize it. These ancient Warriors fused the intense meditation practices of Zen Buddhism with death-defying physical activity (swordplay). Through this fusion, they inadvertently produced the perfect atmosphere for the brain to manufacture the most powerful drugs on the planet (norepinephrine, dopamine, anandamide, serotonin, and endorphins). This powerful combination of a non-dual state derived from meditation and intense focused action initiated the flow state whenever and wherever these Warriors wished. If they can do it, why can't we?

Flow enables anyone to perform at ultra-human performance levels and to transcend their egoic constraints and fear of death. It is also my estimation that this attainment (with slightly different chemical alterations in the brain) is incredibly similar to Christ consciousness. These superhuman states are readily available to anyone willing to dedicate themselves to the mystical path. They are also the gateway to unrealized human potential, union with our Heavenly Father, and true joy on an unprecedented scale.

Kotler's quote, powerful and precisely true, is worth reading again. This time, as you read it, let it soak in, and ask the Holy Spirit if indeed the words both I and Kotler have drafted are true.

"With our sense of self out of the way, we are liberated from doubt and insecurity. With time gone, there is no yesterday to regret or tomorrow to worry about. And when our sense of space disappears, so do physical consequences. But when all three vanish at once, something far more incredible occurs: our fear of death—that most fundamental of all fears—can no longer exist. Simply put: if you are infinite and atemporal, you cannot die."

CHAPTER TWELVE

Fishing from the Wrong Side of the Boat:

The Phenomena of the Left and Right Brain

"Yin and Yang are the two opposites which control the universe and thus the human body."
—George Lucas

L et me say again that we cannot interpret scripture nor anything of spiritual value through the left hemisphere of the brain. The brain is split down the middle by the inter-hemispheric fissure. In actuality, the left and right hemispheres of the brain are so vastly different they may as well belong to different people. The qualities of the left hemisphere of the brain are dualistic, categorizing, logical, and analytical. The left side of the brain likes routine and repetition. The right side of the brain houses non-dual awareness, emotional intelligence, imagination, abstractness, and our omnipresent spiritual radar detector. The Holy Bible is filled with innuendo, or Koan-like inferences, concerning this reality.

Adam and Eve are the left and right sides or "Yin and Yang" of God's creation. The female right is chaos to the order of the male left. One of my favorite scriptures is an obscure passage in John: 21:4-7, which seems to have gone largely unnoticed for 2000 years. Following the Resurrection, Jesus visits with His disciples for a third time. They are fishing not far offshore when suddenly they see a man walking along the water. He is shouting at them, asking if they have had any luck catching fish. Please keep in mind, "fishing" is a constant metaphor in the New Testament. So much so, the fish symbol or *Ichthus* became the secret sign of the early Christian Church.

Anything to do with fishing in the first four books of the New Testament are metaphors, or Koans, enticing us to dig or "fish" deeper into our right brain for the hidden meaning of certain scripture. In this passage, the apostles do not recognize Jesus (another thread running through the four Gospels of Matthew, Mark, Luke and John, concerning Jesus' resurrection). This thread is also commonly dismissed by theologians, but I believe it to be yet another metaphor, or Koan, inviting us to look a bit deeper into its hidden meaning.

John 21:4-7 (NIV) seems like biblical filler at first glance, but no word or sentence in the entire Bible is without layers of wisdom and hidden meaning. *"He called out to them, "Friends, haven't you any fish?' 'No' they answered. He said, "Throw your net on the right side of the boat and you will find some."*

Could we deduce that the biblical translation of the apostles' inability to recognize Jesus means we cannot realize Christ consciousness from the left side of the brain? Is Jesus saying in yet another parable that we are *fishing* on the wrong side of the boat or brain?

This may seem bizarre at first, but I assure you this assumption and logical conclusion is profound to say the least. If we deduce this to be true, then we are also implying that 2000 years ago, Jesus knew that the spiritual data center, the brain, was split in half. One half, the logical computing system, is completely dedicated to the chores of daily living and is subservient to the flesh. The other acts as the spiritual radar detector and assimilator required to glimpse the vastness of our Heavenly Father. I find this assumption to be valid due to the fact current science is just now proving, through quantum mechanics, what mystics have been saying for the last 6000 years: the cosmos is one interconnected and interdependent organism. I think it is highly probable Jesus not only understood the dilemma of our biology, but also the corresponding solution to higher states of consciousness.

The apostles were "fishing" on the left side of the boat and were not catching anything. They were also running from the Roman authorities and living in tomorrow, a perpetual state of fear and anxiety housed on the left side of the brain. Living in the future causes massive amounts of fear and anxiety, which Kotler and ancient samurai declared to be the enemy of human performance and spiritual awakening. Is it possible this seemingly obscure passage is telling us that, while the left hemisphere of the brain serves in practical daily living, it is absolutely worthless to catch "fish"? Is tapping into the right brain and its qualities necessary to attain union with God or to become Superman? I think so, but judge for yourself. As you continue reading, I encourage you to quiet the left hemisphere of the brain and shift to the right. One good way to know the difference is when this book begins to challenge your beliefs. Belief is to stand on the sure-footed safety of the shore, attached to terra firma, while gazing at the distant horizon. Faith is the letting go of self and egoic delusion then diving headfirst into the abyss, all the while knowing our Heavenly Father will always have our back. For the remainder of *The Total Warrior*, I highly encourage you to cast your net, and never look back.

CHAPTER THIRTEEN

Developing the 7th Sense: Discernment

"God never gives us discernment in order that we may criticize, but that we may intercede."
—**Oswald Chambers**

M orihei Ueshiba, commonly known as O'Sensei, was one of the greatest, most enlightened Warriors of all time. The founder of Aikido, he frequently spoke of, not five, but *seven* senses. The first five senses are sight, hearing, touch, taste, and sight. The sixth sense is the gift of extra-sensory perception as we open ourselves to the Holy Spirit. The seventh sense is the next stage in the evolution of Christ consciousness. In Christianity, this sense is referred to as *discernment*. I want to expound on Webster's definition of discernment, which is perception in the absence of judgment with a view to obtaining spiritual direction and understanding. Discernment becomes more evident as we cleanse our minds of the unconscious clutter and the ever-pervasive attacks of darkness. Now, there is energy and the ability to channel and focus our combined mental/spiritual energies toward the attainment of Christ consciousness.

As opposed to ignoring or tempering the six senses, which can individually overwhelm us, we should instead channel them into one central collection point. This collection point is discernment, or the seventh sense. When all six senses are funneled into the seventh, we gain what many call "spiritual goggles," massive powers of observation into the past, present, and future. Through this holy power of observation, we begin to see the inner working of the universe, the principles that underlie all things, and how they are inter-connected. We can clearly see and feel truth, both internal and external, in our minds as it arises. This process is much like watching our lives play out on a giant movie screen complete with pause, fast forward, and rewind buttons.

We are now capable of acting and using *free will*, which is liberated from the bondage of the unconscious mind and dark forces. Without discernment, we have no access to the weapons required to fight the spiritual war constantly being waged around us.

This war is not fought in open fields, triple-canopy jungles, nor the rolling sand dunes of the harshest deserts. Spiritual warfare takes place in our minds and the minds of our loved ones.

"Finally, be strong in the Lord and in his mighty power. Put on the full armor of God, so that you can take your stand against the devil's schemes. For our struggle is not against flesh and blood, but against the rulers, against the authorities, against the powers of this dark world and against the spiritual forces of evil in the heavenly realms. Therefore, put on the full armor of God, so that when the day of evil comes, you may be able to stand your ground, and after you have done everything, to stand. Stand firm then, with the belt of truth buckled around your waist, with the breastplate of righteousness in place, and with your feet fitted with the readiness that comes from the gospel of peace. In addition to all this, take up the shield of faith, with which you can extinguish all the flaming arrows of the evil one. Take the helmet of salvation and the sword of the Spirit, which is the word of God. And pray in the Spirit on all occasions with all kinds of prayers and requests. With this in mind, be alert and always keep on praying for all the Lord's people." (Ephesians 6:10-18 NIV)

Even if spiritual warfare manifests into physical disease (which it absolutely can), it always originates in the unconscious mind. Careful consideration should be paid to the endless enemies at the gate of our minds. These enemies can include, but are not limited to, the shared unconscious mind, our egos, and especially, evil forces. There is a war constantly being waged for the possession of your soul, through your mind. The weapons the dark enemy uses to control your mind are the addiction to the five senses, addiction to earthly forms and the emotions they produce, such as fear, regret, unworthiness, anger, hatred, jealousy, resentment, and greed.

Although Satan's name "Accuser" has changed many times throughout history, the evil he and his fellow fallen angels embody has been with us since time immemorial. Revelation 12:9 (ESV) tells us, "*And the great dragon was thrown down, that ancient serpent, who is called the devil and Satan, the deceiver of the whole world—he was thrown down to the earth, and his angels were thrown down with him.*"

Strangely, little is spoken of Satan in the Old Testament where he is almost always seen as a serpent, dragon, or the Evil One. He is not personified until the ministry of Jesus in the New

Testament and, more specifically, during the three temptations of Christ during the forty days and forty nights in the desert.

I want to be perfectly clear on this point. Both the good and evil forces waging spiritual warfare cannot be comprehended through the five senses nor the left hemisphere of the brain. These are the very vehicles evil forces use to wage their war against us, therefor a shift from logic to illumined imagination (dream state), combined with discernment, is the only way to understand both evil and divine forces. Outside of this coupling, we have no possible means of grasping the true essence of spirit entities, such as angels or demons (much like we will never fully embody the vast, infinite, omnipresence of God while in human form).

Both good and evil spirits unquestionably exist and can take the form of anything they choose, such as animals, nature, or human beings. Another important point is that, while these forces exist, we cannot lay the entire blame for our conduct or our health, or that of our loved ones, conveniently at the feet of Satan. I tend to think of both evil and divine forces being like radio waves that are constantly present in the heavens. If your radio is out of tune, it gets nothing but chaos and static (i.e., evil). If, on the other hand, your radio is dialed in with hi-fi capacity and your antenna fully erect, divine forces are free to enter and begin their work.

Time and time again, the New Testament illustrates how Jesus cast out demons. For instance, both Mark 5:1-20 and Luke 8:26-39 go into detail concerning the Gadarene, a devil-possessed man who lived a most bizarre lifestyle. The Gadarene lived amongst tombs. He howled, cut himself with stones, ran around naked, and had bursts of amazing strength, which apparently enabled him to break chains. Pay special attention to how

Jesus addressed the unclean spirit in the Gadarene, *"What is thy name?"* and how the spirit responded, *"My name is Legion: for we are many."* The demons beg Jesus not to cast them into the flaming pit of hell but into a herd of wild pigs instead. Jesus gladly obliges and sends them off a cliff and into a lake, drowning them to death.

My aim in discussing spiritual warfare is twofold. First, for far too long a large percentage of the Christian church has conveniently focused an extreme amount of effort combating and blaming the devil for all improprieties, especially if it directly involves the Church. While the Saturday Night Live church lady was funny in the 80s, there is no longer any room or patience amongst sober followers of Jesus for hellfire and brimstone sermons or fear mongering of any kind. Relative to this claim, let me share a personal anecdote.

Recently, I worked with a ministry for veterans. The leader of the organization verbally assaulted me for patting him on the back and saying good morning. Apparently, he believed demons might jump into his body if touched by another person. Not only does this border on insanity, it could also have caused serious damage had he unleashed his verbal assault on a wounded veteran still fragile from the trauma of war and the effects of PTSD.

In moving forward, we must gain better vision through discernment and view the world with spiritual goggles. This vantage point allows us to clearly see the forces of evil at play and disseminate them from psychological psychosis, mental illness, or a complete lack of moral aptitude. As followers of Jesus, we must become apologists who provide truthful, biblical answers to exceedingly difficult questions pertaining to the gospel. We must stop the "kitchen table" Christianity, which is not based solely on the gospel and return to *grace*, through faith in Christ.

When we assign blame to Satan for all things wrong with the world, we lose personal responsibility for our actions and any ability to rectify these actions. God wants and requires a relationship with us. This especially applies to spiritual warfare and our willingness to see the profound difference between falling short of our own merits and knowing when the Angel of Darkness has invaded our hearts and minds.

As followers of Jesus, we must all become men of the cloth, fully capable of donning the armor of God and dispensing with the devil at will. We must trust in and then let go of these abilities just as we would trust a vehicle to carry us down the highway without constantly worrying whether the wheels are going to fall off. We cannot live a life of fear thinking the Devil is under every rock or an evil spirit might consume us because we bumped into someone at Walmart. Jesus has given us the authority to do all things in His name, and He is Lord of lords and King of kings on Earth and in Heaven (Matthew 28:16-20).

All that is needed is the discernment to know when it's time to draw our swords and when it is time to keep them sheathed.

John 14:12-14 (NIV) reads, "*Very truly I tell you, whoever believes in me will do the works I have been doing, and they will do even greater things than these, because I am going to the Father. And I will do whatever you ask in my name, so that the Father may be glorified in the Son. You may ask me for anything in my name, and I will do it.*"

The closer you fly to the sun, the harsher the attacks from Satan. Never lose sight of Jesus as He wanders forty days and forty nights through the desert sands, combating Satan every step of the way, armed only with the Word of God. Denounce all assignments with Satan and the brokenness of your left brain. Work every day to remove your addictions to the five senses and earthly forms so that the false self, or ego, slowly dwindles and, with it, Satan's only chance to defeat you in the greatest battle of your life.

CHAPTER FOURTEEN

The Importance of
Positive Self-Talk

**"The more man meditates upon good thoughts,
the better will be his world and the world at large."
—Confucius**

If the mind is the vehicle Satan uses to attack us, then
unconscious thinking and, more specifically, "self-talk" is
his infantry. A vast majority of our self-talk is negative. We
hardly ever have thoughts of positive reinforcement, such as
"you got this," "you're amazing," or "God loves you just the
way you are." Only Stuart Smiley, the eternal optimist from
Saturday Night Live had such fortune. For the rest of us, self-
talk is a daily mental barrage, making us feel unworthy, alone,
and afraid.

As we increase our prayer and meditation practice, these
voices will lessen and create space for Christ consciousness.
Unfortunately, those negative voices may never totally sub-
side. As our conscious attention increases, we will notice these
voices the instant they arise. When they do, we must draw our

swords and slash them to pieces with this simple and incredibly effective prayer:

"In the name and authority of Jesus Christ, I silence all voices except God Almighty, His Son Jesus Christ, and the Holy Spirit."

As silly as it may seem, once these voices have been silenced, follow them with a concerted effort of positive reinforcement and self-talk. Say something like, "I am worthy of God's love," "I am a good person," and "I can do all things through Jesus Christ." Or try the ancient Stoic practice of saying to yourself, "I love this," or "I chose this" during high stress moments when it appears things are not going your way.

It should never be lost on us that we are having conversation with ourselves. Who is talking? Who is listening? How many of us are in there? Gaining objective distance from the internal voices and viewing them from a detached "true self" is a practice of shifting from dual consciousness into a non-dual or Christ consciousness state. Sit, and observe your mind as these voices come into view. Once you begin to see them from the mountain peak, they tend to run and hide from the immense light cast upon them.

During your meditation practice, once the mind has been quieted, a highly effective practice is to form a question and then "look" for the answer. Pose the question to yourself, "What is my next thought?" Say it multiple times and then "look" for the thought to materialize. Notice the vast space and emptiness that accompanies this exercise. Try to remain in this emptiness for longer periods of time with ever-increasing awareness of both internal and external environments, especially thoughts as they appear and disappear.

CHAPTER FIFTEEN

Post-Traumatic Stress Disorder

*"Trauma is hell on earth. Trauma resolved is
a gift from the gods."*
—Peter A. Levine

In his book *Tribe,* Sebastian Junger offers a frank and data-driven hypothesis as to the primary contributor to PTSD among veterans. Contrary to popular belief, the main contributor is not always related to physical combat experiences. In fact, many soldiers experiencing PTSD never saw a single day of combat nor experienced any type of life-threatening training, such as Airborne, Ranger, or even Air Assault schools. So, what could cause this phenomenon? Junger suggests that the answer lies in the loss of their *Tribe.*

In Genesis 2:18 (NIV), the Lord says, *"It is not good for the man to be alone."* We, as humans, are social creatures, and we, as men, require the attention, affection, and admiration of other men. Nowhere is this more evident than with the tribe that is created in the combat arms elements of the United States military.

I can personally attest to the tremendous loss I experienced over the fifteen years of absence from my band of brothers, my *tribe*. Something incredibly special happens when men join in shared mindset and vision, especially when their lives are on the line. The individual ego begins to fade and love for your brother becomes the central focus. This focus overrides any sense of selfishness or egoic concern. As the self is lost to the greater whole, a sense of peace, trust, and duty take root. For most of us, this cannot be replaced in civilian life. This loss of tribe can be catastrophic to the individual and must be restored with a sense of priority. The tribe can be replicated with the joining and willful participation of a church, veterans' group, outreach ministry, or all the above.

Not only are we made to be in a tribe, but we're also made to be of service. There is no greater way to live our lives than to combine a sense of *tribe* with an all-out commitment of service to our fellow brothers and sisters.

Another contributing factor to PTSD is the "story." Everyone has a story, a narrative in which you are either the protagonist or antagonist (depending on how much BS or self-torture you offer your "self"). The story is just that—a story. The problem is, the story gets stuck, not only in our minds but in our bodies. This "stuckness" can become both a mental and physical disease as it abscesses over time. Critical attention must be paid to the removing of this abscess before it becomes systemic. The only way to carve this disease out of our existence is to tell our story, sometimes over and over, until it loses its power and grip on our souls. The telling of the story objectifies and shines light where only darkness once thrived.

This darkness is fertile soil for Satan and his minions to carry out horrible crimes against us and take full possession of the soul. Seeking out qualified spiritual or psychological counselors to aid in the exorcism of the story demon is an absolute essential exercise that must take place for anyone suffering from PTSD to find peace. This requires massive levels of trust and a dedication to achieving the peace of mind you must believe in your heart is deserved.

Our stories are just that, stories. They have no intrinsic power. We—and possibly evil forces—weaponize our past and turns it against us. The greatest way to end this threat is to realize you are not your story. You are not your past. You are the eyes of God, waiting to be realized.

CHAPTER SIXTEEN

The Law of Attraction

"You create your thoughts; your thoughts create your intentions, and your intentions create your reality."
—Wayne Dyer

Our souls dwell in three states of consciousness:

- The Waking State, where we come in contact with the shared experience of reality as it unfolds in God's creation. All of creation is the physical manifestation of the Mind of God. On an EEG, the alpha and beta brain-wave patterns of the Waking State resemble the Himalayan Mountains with extremely high peaks and valleys.

- The Dream State—the daily experience of our souls being liberated from the shackles of the flesh and the external realm of physical creation, which includes our own bodies. Dreams are the abstract component of the Mind of God, a borderless place where the seed of infinite possibility can take root in the physical creation.

The theta Dream State brain waves look much like soft, rolling hills.

- The Conscious State—a deep, dreamless sleep of pure emptiness—displays a delta brain-wave pattern and is as close to a flatline as you can get shy of death. In this state, "no-thing" is arising, an utter and total emptiness, the bare essence of our Maker. Every night as we sleep, our souls rest in this emptiness, free of all form (i.e., thoughts and dreams). This Conscious State is the purest form of the soul and is the timeless realm of ever present "nowness," where we connect with our Maker. It is here our bodies find healing and restorative power. Without deep, dreamless sleep, the delta brain wave pattern and the sustenance found within, the human organism will deteriorate within twenty-four hours and expire within seven to ten days.

The other method of obtaining the theta dream state and delta wave patterns is through the practice of meditation. Meditation is the deepest method of prayer and is also the cornerstone for developing the mindset of the Warrior. Meditation practice fosters true discipline and wisdom. It molds the mind into a finely tuned instrument, with which the Warrior may properly affect his world. As we sit in deeper levels of consciousness, we free ourselves from the bondage of the flesh and our broken minds. For a moment, we dwell in the Mind of God Himself and the profound experience of "I Am-ness." Proverbs 4:6 (NIV) tells us, "Do not forsake wisdom, and she will protect you; love her, and she will watch over you."

Wisdom is the gateway to discernment. Through discernment, we can judge how best to live our lives and how to make the daily decisions that either bring us closer to our Heavenly Father or push us further away. As we mold our minds into tools to be used for divine purpose, the practice of "right-mindedness"—the conscious control of every thought flowing through our minds—becomes natural and effortless.

Many books, such as The Secret and Think and Grow Rich by Napoleon Hill, outline the importance of generating positive thoughts, which attract to us the people, places, and opportunities to make our dreams come true. This is not a fallacy; it is how reality manifests itself. The universe is constantly conspiring to bring to you the abundance of God's love, but, in our fallen state, our minds are not our own and cannot connect to nor manifest the riches that await us all.

Our outer lives are a symbol of the internal practice (or lack thereof) of controlling and manipulating our thoughts. There is no external action ever taken that does not originate in the mind as a thought form. If you don't think about it first, you cannot go to the bathroom and sit on a toilet. Every action or inaction is preceded by a thought and, quite possibly, the overwhelming emotion that accompanies it.

The "secret" is to understand how the universe truly manifests itself, and then embody the amazing, untapped power you have over your life and the lives of your loved ones. I have outlined a very simple process that should become a daily practice to be performed before bedtime.

Nightly Visualization Prayer

First, lie in bed, arms at your side, palms facing up. Begin to breath mindfully, relaxing the body and slowing the heart rate. Place in your mind a specific vision of yourself experiencing whatever your heart desires. For instance, if you are seeking healing, focus on that specific issue and see yourself being completely healed. If it is for monetary benefit, see yourself as you would be if you were financially secure and truly free of the worry and stress money places on your life. Whatever your dream may be, focus on yourself living in that experience. The more vivid and detailed, the better.

Now, this is the most critical element to the practice. How does the vision feel? What are the emotions you are experiencing? Focus on those emotions, especially the feeling of gratitude. Gratitude is the honey that attracts the bees that pollinate the flower of your dreams. Gratitude is the most powerful, transformational emotion in our toolchest and is the gateway to peace and joy. Happiness is a momentary, situational experience, which is fleeting at best. Joy is eternal. Joy is the everlasting gift of God's love and the true abundance offered of a life lived in Christ consciousness.

The next morning, once you awake, write down in detail what the vision was about. From there, create a list of goals based on that vision. Again, if the vision is healing, what are the goals that would lead to healing? For instance:

Goal #1 – I am going to exercise thirty minutes every day.

Goal #2 – I am going to pray for healing five times every day.

Goal #3 – I will focus only on healing thoughts

Goal #4 – I will seek out physicians who see me as a human being and not a broken widget.

Goal #5 – I will use food as a medicine, not as an escape or intoxicant.

The same goal-setting process should be put in place no matter what your vision may be. Try to be as specific as possible by using the S.M.A.R.T. goal acronym. S.M.A.R.T. goals are:

1. Specific

2. Measurable

3. Achievable

4. Relevant

5. Time bound

The more attention you place on creating SMART goals, the higher the possibility of attaining those goals. Each morning as you read through your goals, once again envision yourself living the experience. Feel the emotion surrounding the vision, focusing on gratitude. Lastly, several times throughout the day, read your goals out loud and place your intention on achieving those goals for that day. Is what you are doing right now part of the plan, or have you drifted away? How can you make a course correction right here, right now? The practice of manifesting our dreams and living a life capable of transformation takes massive commitment, practice, and discipline.

Putting a "W" or "Win" in the column for each and every day is the ultimate goal of this practice. Without a doubt, the single greatest threat to success is starting over and over and over again. Groundhog Day is one of my favorite movies, but it's not a great way to live life. Every day must be seen as the battle it is, and the only way to victory is to carpe diem—seize the day! I call the process of daily wins "dry stacking."

Dry stacking refers to a building technique using concrete blocks with no mortar between them. The surface on both sides of the blocks is coated with a special high-strength cement creating a "sandwich" effect that is stronger than a typical mortar joint.

Consistent discipline is the key to dry stacking. Its absence can result in a man's downfall and defeat. For those who have experienced lives of discipline, such as that of former military or a competitive athlete, this defeat is cataclysmic, especially when he later on in life finds himself at the mercy of alcohol, drugs, sex, or insidious food. The worst kind of death is having to constantly start over and dealing with the resulting feeling of failure. It is a death of a thousand cuts and a form of hell on earth. The world needs men to be who God created us to be. We become the best versions of ourselves, capable of living lives pleasing to God, through diligent and intentional daily practice. It doesn't happen involuntarily or by accident.

CHAPTER SEVENTEEN

Utility and Longevity of the Brain

"The Pen is Mightier than the sword."
—Edward Bulwer-Lytton

T he brain is primarily a muscle. (Well, it's mostly fat, but you get my point.) If we don't train the muscle, we will lose its capabilities. With our reliance on technology and our inability to critically think for ourselves, our culture is slowly reverting to ape-like levels of cognitive aptitude. Daily practice must be taken to exercise the mind, especially in these areas:

- reading and comprehension

- writing

- critical thinking

- effective communication

- problem solving

- focus and attention

- memory capacity

God crafted our amazing brains to be capable of painting the Mona Lisa, landing man on the moon, and even sitting in His presence. Much attention should be paid to the essential tools needed for development of both the left and right hemispheres of the brain. Learning how to critically think and write are the two most powerful weapons anyone can possess. Today, for some reason, we are failing to inform our children (and society) that these critical skills are the sole reason for attending university.

Pour yourself into study and force yourself into writing. Start a personal blog or post something heartfelt and inspirational every day on social media.

We learn and teach through three vehicles: logic, imagination, and application. These are also the vehicles of apologetics. Reading, writing, and debating are the most effective means of training the brain to perform its two most important functions, how to effectively think (i.e., dream, vision, intention, and set goals) and communicate those thoughts (*"The Word became flesh ..." John 1:14*). Social media can be a powerful and simple tool to practice the apologetics of our faith, while exercising the greatest gift of God's creation: our brains.

CHAPTER EIGHTEEN

Spiritual Warfare

"Spiritual warfare is very real. There is a furious, fierce, and ferocious battle raging in the realm of the spirit between the forces of God and the forces of evil. Warfare happens every day, all the time. Whether you believe it or not, you are in a battlefield. You are in warfare."
—Pedro Okoro

In the first centuries of the Christian Church, a small sect of monks, known as the Desert Fathers, emerged in Egypt. Perhaps as early as the late 200s AD, these Egyptian Christian men left the pagan cities and the persecutions and the distractions of life to live as hermits in the Sahara Desert. Their purpose was to live a solitary life solely dedicated to God and to be on the front lines of the greatest battle of all. They were uniquely chosen from among the strongest monks, much like professional athletes today, to live a hermetic life of solitude and to do battle with Satan himself.

This war was not fought in the endless shifting desert sands, but inside the minds and hearts of men, alone in dark caves, in constant prayer and meditation. Their purpose was not only to

177

reach the pinnacle of spiritual achievement, but to wage war on darkness and, simultaneously, raise the entire *consciousness* of man. The Desert Fathers sacrificed all to walk the razor's edge of faith for the soul purpose of achieving union with God and increasing the possibility of this union for those of us willing to follow. The same is true for our efforts, should we choose to join them in this battle.

As modern-day Warriors, we must plant the seeds offered us through inspired grace. We must tend our internal gardens so that righteous fruit may grow. We must learn to see the shared principles underlying the foundations of nature and the awe-inspiring potential of our human form upon re-birth. We must learn to feel and hear the Holy spirit and act on His wisdom. We must be willing to expand our minds and discover the endless ways this wisdom attempts to speak to us. These ways include nature, art, music, and the writings of mystical traditions fused with true science, which has its basis in the written word. We must be equally equipped in apologetics and sound biblical theology to defend God's Word against charlatans, non-believers, and Satan's minions.

We must be willing to go to war. By this I mean we must be willing to kill, and we must be willing to die. This war is a spiritual war, and the killing and dying is in surrendering our*selves* and being willing to die for our neighbor. You are not alone in this fight. Your sword and shield will be the knowledge you have gained through the divine writings of the ancient saints, the Holy Bible, and the authority granted you by Jesus Christ.

Lastly, or perhaps firstly, Jesus is Lord!

Never forget that Jesus, and Jesus alone, is Lord of all lords and King of all kings. All laws, and representatives of the law, are subservient to the law of Jesus Christ and His Great Commission as stated in Mathew 28:16-20 (KJV):

"Then the eleven disciples went away into Galilee, into a mountain where Jesus had appointed them. And when they saw him, they worshiped him: but some doubted. And Jesus came and spake unto them, saying, All power is given unto me in heaven and in earth. Go ye therefore, and teach all nations, baptizing them in the name of the Father, and of the Son, and of the Holy Ghost: Teaching them to observe all things whatsoever I have commanded you: and, lo, I am with you always, [even] unto the end of the world. Amen."

As Warriors, we must carry this knowledge with us everywhere. We must never let fear or concern for ourselves outweigh our Christian duty to uphold His Law.

Never has humanity faced the type of darkness we see rising among us today. This darkness (Satan) will attack you, your family, friends, and loved ones the second you step on the Christian path. The more you grow in His light, the more intense the attacks will be. Never turn your back or let down your guard. Never let fear or worry consume your heart, body, and mind. As you take up the armor of God and ready yourself for battle, know your brothers fight beside you, and no man will ever be left behind. Never forget the lineage to which you now belong. Hold tight to the fervent belief that only the few, filled with faith and the glory of God, can do the impossible.

CHAPTER NINETEEN

Following the Warrior Path

"Finally, my brethren, be strong in the Lord and in the power of His might. Put on the whole armor of God, that you may be able to stand against the wiles of the devil. For we do not wrestle against flesh and blood, but against principalities, against powers, against the rulers of the darkness of this age, against spiritual hosts of wickedness in the heavenly places. Therefore take up the whole armor of God, that you may be able to withstand in the evil day, and having done all, to stand."
—Ephesians 6:10-13

Only through the strongest desire imaginable is it possible to achieve union with God. The Christian Warrior must put God before everything, including yourself, your family, job, reputation, and ambition. Know and live His Gospel. Be prepared to defend the Gospel and the Five Solas with fierce knowledge of His Word. In this chapter, I want to give you eight other steps the Warrior must take in order to achieve his full potential. They are:

1. Dig in!

The Warrior's first line of defense is to cultivate stillness of mind and non-dual consciousness through fervent meditation and contemplative prayer. (See the following chapter.)

2. Gain the high ground.

We are only free to exercise free will and gain relationship with our Heavenly Father after we have breached the unconscious mind and the confines of the ego. While we remain in the darkness of the mind, we are subject to the attacks from evil forces and the addiction of our own flesh.

3. Form an objective opinion of your "self."

- What are my addictions to earthly possessions and/ or things?

- What sins does my ego use to keep me shackled and how are they expressed?

- How can I stay mindful and aware of my ego as it falls back into darkness?

- Learn to receive forgiveness when you stumble. Stay objective.

4. Ask "What would Jesus do?"

In Jesus we have been given a perfect example of how we are to live our best lives. It is His prayer that we would walk with Him daily, living each moment in gratitude for His sacrifice and unconditional love for us. As a Warrior, immerse yourself in the joy springing from your newly found freedom and faith in Christ. Pick up your own cross and walk beside him *in living faith*. Put your life into the hands of our Heavenly Father and live for His glory, not your own.

5. The Body is the Temple.

If you have made it this far in the book and believe in the words I have written, then you know in your heart the profoundness of this statement. Do not forget it. Every breath you take, water you drink, food you eat, every thought you think endlessly creates the *"Christbody"* your soul inhabits. Apply your best efforts to remove all impurities, such as alcohol, and all mind/body-altering chemicals. Continuously cleanse yourself like a glacial lake, capable of reflecting the awesomeness of our Father and His Son Jesus Christ.

Your body is the creation and the home of God Himself. Treat it as such!

6. Love your neighbor as yourself.

Jesus tells us the second greatest commandment is to love your neighbor as yourself. This is a parable and is meant to be a bit of a riddle. Its purpose is for us to begin the process of looking inside ourselves. How do we love ourselves? If it is through the judging eye of dual consciousness, then we will see our neighbor through this same judging eye. Every human on the planet is a soul, inhabiting a body just like you. Our souls are like waves on the ocean, seemingly separate and different but all part of the same ocean. Never forget you and all forms arising in every moment are impermanent and in constant state of transformation. Only the soul residing in Christ was born again and, because of that re-birth, will never die.

Learn to see through the eyes of Christ as Heaven on Earth materializes in infinite nowness.

7. Never allow your sword to rust.

As Warriors of the light, we have a bound duty to train and purify our hearts, minds, souls, and bodies. If we never draw our swords, they will rust inside their scabbards and become worthless. You must sacrifice a part of yourself every day to rigorous training if you expect to do battle with the angel of darkness and his minions.

- Constantly expand your brain's cognitive abilities through reading, writing, communication, and critical thinking.

- Strengthen your body through anatomical adaptation and physical training.

- Live through prayer and meditation.

- Consistently offer your service to your neighbor.

- Train fervently in self-defense and survival skillsets.

Satan takes no off days; he does not complain, and he does not whine. Rid yourself of excuses and all attachments keeping you from achieving your true potential. Treat every day as an epic battle. Meet it with serious commitment. Take nothing for granted.

8. See the world through spiritual goggles.

Before going to war, it's best to know your enemy. Darkness is pervasive, porous, and resides deep inside your heart and the hearts of our brothers and sisters. We are wicked sinners, and only through Christ may we rise out of our fallen state.

Before setting out to do battle, fight the demon residing inside you first. When you begin to see the darkness residing inside your own heart and mind, you will quickly recognize it in others.

Satan weaves his evil through the acts of man. These acts arise in the form of our government, schools, businesses, institutions, and even churches. It is imperative that the Warrior learn to listen and trust his gut when something doesn't *feel* right. Armed with the wisdom of the ancient Warriors and saints, and with the Trinity at your side, you are an Army of one. Live in this truth, for it will become your shield.

The cultivation of the Warrior Spirit and a new term you will soon learn to embody, *Christ Consciousness*, is best approached through three distinctive practices:

Morning Prayer

Father, wash me in the blood of your son Jesus Christ
Cleanse my heart, body, and soul that your Holy spirit may dwell in me
Place the Helmet of Salvation upon my head so that Satan can never again attack my mind, my thoughts, my dreams, my visions, or my emotions

Place the Breastplate of Righteousness over my heart, fill it with love, compassion, gratitude, and joy

Tie the belt of Faith around my waist, my lord, that I may be sanctified in your Word

Let me step into the shoes of Jesus Christ, open my eyes to the works you placed upon me, lend me your strength and courage oh lord, as I join my lord and Savior

Jesus Christ and walk hand in hand beside Him

Place your mighty shield in my left-hand lord that I might protect myself, my loved ones and all your children lord from the darkness of the enemy

Give to me the sword of light, Father, that I may cast it into the dark heart of Satan wherever and whenever he crosses my path

In the name and Authority of Jesus Christ I pray,
Amen

Effective Prayer

Effective prayer is an internal or external, verbal conversation we know God hears. David wrote in *Psalm 34:15, 17-18.* *"The eyes of the LORD are on the righteous, and His ears are open to their cry.... The righteous cry out, and the LORD hears, and delivers them out of all their troubles. The LORD is near to those who have a broken heart and saves such as have a contrite spirit"*.

Effective prayer is an ongoing dialogue with and through the Trinity. It is an opening of your heart and a pleading to the Father to know Him better and for Him to guide, support and protect you and your loved ones as you walk the path of Jesus

Christ. Here is an example of an effective prayer I say every morning over my wife:

Father, give to us this day
Cleanse our bodies, minds and souls Father, that your Holy Spirit may dwell in us
Father we pray for healing. We pray you remove all illness, sickness, and disease
Fill our hearts with love, joy and gratitude
Fill our minds with your infinite wisdom
Shine the light of your kingdom on the path of our lord and savior Jesus Christ
Open our eyes to the works you have placed before us
Give us your strength and Courage, O Lord, that we may join your Son and walk with Him, hand in hand
Father we pray that darkness be lifted and the light of your kingdom shine into the hearts and minds of our brothers and sisters
In the name and Authority of Jesus Christ, I pray

Welcoming Prayer

Father Thomas Keating instructs practitioners of Centering Prayer in his classic work on the contemplative dimension of the Gospel, *Open Mind, Open Heart*. The Welcoming Prayer is a method of consenting to God's presence and action in our physical and emotional reactions to events and situations in daily life. The purpose of the Welcoming Prayer is to deepen our relationship with God through consenting in ordinary activities like breathing. The Welcoming Prayer helps to dismantle the emotional programs of the false self-system and to heal the wounds of a lifetime by addressing them where they are stored — in the body. It contributes to the process of transformation in Christ initiated in contemplative prayer. The practice of Welcoming Prayer is an opportunity to make choices free of the false-self system — responding instead of reacting to the present moment. Through the action of the Holy Spirit, our practice empowers us to take appropriate action as freely and lovingly as possible in any situation that presents itself in our lives.

Example of Welcoming Prayer

With a full, deep inhalation, say the following:

I am breathing in, the Holy, Healing Spirit of my Lord Jesus Christ

(Hold the inhalation and "sit" in the "fullness" of the experience)
(Slowly, breathe out and say:)

I am breathing out all illness, sickness, and disease
All darkness, evil and sin
All attachment to my five senses
All attachment to earthly things

(Pause with the full exhale and "sit" with the "emptiness" of the experience)
Continue this prayer until a sense of peace and stillness consumes you. Sit in this presence for as long as possible with a full sense of gratitude.

Lectio Divina

Lectio Divina is a contemplative way of reading the Bible. It dates back to the early centuries of the Christian Church and was established as a monastic practice by Benedict in the 6th century. It is a way of praying the scriptures that leads us deeper into God's word. We slow down. We read a short passage more than once. We chew it over slowly and carefully. We savor it. Scripture begins to speak to us in a new way. It speaks to us personally and aids that union we have with God through Christ, the Living Word.

Friar Christopher Jamison, former Abbot of Worth Abbey in Sussex, England, in his book *Finding Sanctuary* writes of three key features of lectio:

- **The first** is that "the text is seen as a gift to be received, not a problem to be dissected...let the text come to you."

- **The second** is that the Lectio tradition teaches us that in order to receive what the text has to offer we must read slowly.

- **The third** is that Lectio is "a way of prayer." Before reading, pray that God will speak to you through the text. During reading, allow the reading to evolve into meditation and then into prayer and finally contemplation. When the reading is concluded, keep some phrase in mind and repeat it throughout the day so that prayerful reading becomes prayerful living.

Contemplative Prayer or Meditation to Foster "Stillness"

The process of contemplative prayer or meditation is a four-step process.

1. **Attention**

   Assume the appropriate sitting position. This can be done sitting on the floor or in a chair. Place the entirety of your single-minded focused "attention" on the spine. Stack the head over the shoulders so no tension arises in the neck. Next, retract your shoulder blades and raise your chest and heart as though exposing it to the heavens. Stack each vertebra one on top of the other in perfect alignment until the weight of your upper torso is securely placed in the hips, and through the hips into the floor. Continue to come back to this attention in a cyclic fashion to ensure proper posture throughout the prayer.

2. **Mindfulness.**

   Inhale deeply through the nose, pause at the top of the breath and release slowly through the mouth and glottis until it makes a bit of a "Darth Vader" type sound. Pause at the bottom of the exhale. Notice the sensation caused by breathing. Notice the expansion and contraction of the body with each breath. Notice the opening of the heart and the slowing of the mind as your breath becomes new and different. Mindfulness is a product of "feeling" as though each breath is the very first and last breath you will ever take.

3. **Awareness**.

As you continue with attention on the spine and mind-fulness of breath, push your awareness 360 degrees around your body. Feel, hear, and notice everything but let it pass as though it is a cloud in the sky. Expand your awareness out into the room and notice how your awareness takes up the entirety of every square inch of space surrounding you. You are now ever-expanding awareness, one with everything.

4. **Full Cycle**.

Attention, mindfulness and then awareness, allow yourself to just sit in "nowness" or perpetual "stillness." Notice all thoughts, sounds, smells or distractions of any kind, as they drift in and out of awareness. As these distractions arise, simply "watch" them and say, "that is just me thinking" and let the distraction drift by like a cloud. After some time, begin to "watch" the "watcher" from a much greater distance. Sitting in emptiness is the contemplative experience and the rise of the nondual, Christ consciousness. Sit in this space as long as possible, knowing you are in the lap of God and walking in the light of his kingdom.

CHAPTER TWENTY

The Way of the Harmonious Spirit

"When mind, body and spirit are in harmony, happiness is the natural result."
—Deepak Chopra

A s I briefly described in the opening paragraphs, during my tenure in the Army, I stumbled across an obscure book entitled, *Aikido and the Harmony of Nature*, written by Mitsugi Saotome. Saotome Sensei, is an Aikido master and a personal student (Uchi Deshi) for over fifteen years of Morihei Ueshiba, commonly known as "O'Sensei," which means "Great Teacher." As I turned the pages and devoured Saotome Sensei's words, something overpowered me. Tears streamed down my cheeks as Sensei shared his poetic anecdotes of life under the tutelage of the last great samurai and, quite possibly, the most enlightened sage in Japanese history. The book rocked me deeply and became the motivating reason for leaving the Army. Within a year of reading that book, I found myself on the mat across from the teacher I would spend the next ten years sacrificing everything for. It was all I needed just to be near him.

Today, Aikido has garnered a somewhat tainted reputation as an ineffective fighting art. This is largely due to a misunderstanding and lack of martial skill of its modern practitioners. In addition, following the death of its greatest teachers, the art has been watered down for commercial purposes.

Aikido, as taught by O'Sensei, demanded the toughest, most aggressive martial artists from across Japan. His early Dojo was affectionately nicknamed "Hell Dojo" for its brutality and serious concern for bodily injury and even death. Each of the Uchi Deshi studying under O'Sensei were lethal, killing machines and masters in various forms of martial arts including Judo, Jiu Jitsu, swordsmanship, and Karate.

The idea of Aikido is that of a Ph.D. in martial arts. Aikido assumes the practitioner is already skilled in striking and grappling arts before stepping on the mat. This has somehow been lost in translation over the years and is the primary reason for the degradation of the art. This was not the case the first ten years I studied Aikido. For example, I had been a wrestler, martial artist, and boxer since age seven. At the ripe old age of twenty-two, I was also a seasoned combat veteran.

During the nineties, when you trained with Saotome Sensei, the mat would be filled with the greatest martial artists in the world, along with some unsavory characters looking for a better way to kick ass (like me). I can testify to the brutal effectiveness of Aikido as a martial art, having survived well over one hundred street fights. Once one has cultivated a decent martial skill level and added about five hard years of true Aikido training, the art can be incredibly brutal on the street and should be avoided at all costs.

But, in my early twenties, I was struggling with PTSD, alcoholism, and drug addiction. I was incredibly dark and constantly shaking my fist at God (which I do not recommend). I wanted to destroy everything I got my hands on. My only goal was to become the world's biggest badass and wreak havoc anywhere I could. There was no healthy way for me to channel this aggression because, in the late 80s and early 90s, the UFC Octagon and mixed martial arts (MMA) did not yet exist. If you wanted to test your mettle, you found the toughest bar in town, got drunk, and smacked the biggest, meanest dude you could find. Simple as that. This attitude eventually landed me in the hospital, beaten to a pulp, and comatose for three days.

I can attest to the transformative qualities of Aikido. As I began training, I would periodically experience tidal waves of emotion, released from years of childhood trauma and my experiences in combat. I lived the life of a starving artist, shacking up in dojos across the country and dedicating each day to fervent practice and meditation. After ten years of religious effort and following Saotome Sensei across the nation on his seminar circuit, I finally had my moment to touch him.

I am a skilled fighter. That being said, it has been more a curse than a gift. In many ways I was born for that one single purpose. However, to touch Saotome Sensei is otherworldly, incredibly emasculating and humbling to a young punk like me. The profound experience of training with Sensei ended my days of barroom brawls and aided in the long, hard road of self-discovery and forgiveness.

Saotome Sensei has no openings or weaknesses, and he knows everything you are going to do before you even think of it. Fighting with him is like assaulting an immovable ghost who unravels your senses and aggression before you come close to touching him. Your efforts become absurd and meaningless, as he sucks your energy into his own until two are one and one is none. Training with Saotome Sensei altered my DNA. I'm sure the same is true for Saotome Sensei and the dozens of other Uchi Deshi who had a deep connection with the founder of Aikido, Morihei Ueshiba.

It is mind-blowing to think of O'Sensei's power given how special and different his students were. There is no warrior in modern history who exemplifies the totality of the Warrior Spirit, Heart, Mind, and Soul more than Morihei Ueshiba, nor will there ever be another O'Sensei.

Morihei Ueshiba (1889-1969), Japan's greatest martial artist, was regarded as the country's strongest man even during his youth. At eighty, O'Sensei could disarm any attacker, down any number of assailants, and pin his strongest students with a single finger. Invincible as a warrior, O'Sensei was also an enlightened mystic and man of peace. His experience as a combat veteran of the Russo-Japanese war left him with deep disdain for fighting, war, and any kind of violence, which seems contraindicative of a samurai warrior.

His contribution to martial arts was *Aikido,* refined over many decades. Aikido's roots are found in the bloodiest and most destructive martial art in Japan, the fighting system of the Emperor's Imperial Guards, Daito Ryu Aiki Jiu jitsu. Every technique in Daito Ryu ends in a kill. O'Sensei's grand vision was to create a martial art in which an attacker was subdued and rendered incapacitated, but not destroyed. This responsibility to care for an attacker was an enlightened principle of Aikido. No art before or after has held to the grand standard that all life must be protected, even that of those who mean to do us harm. Simply put, Aikido philosophy should be the martial way of the Christian warrior.

Aikido means the way of harmonious spirit. Unlike Sun Tzu's *The Art of War* and Miyamoto Masashi's *Book of Five Rings*, which accept the inevitability of war and emphasize strategy to obtain victory, O'Sensei intuited that fruitless fighting with others, ourselves, and the environment will only guarantee the destruction of the human species and eventually the earth itself.

O'Sensei taught the art of peace as a creative mind-body discipline, a practical means of conflict resolution and a means of conducting ourselves in personal relationships, society, and nature. O'Sensei's belief was that anyone can, and everyone should, be a warrior for peace. His prayer was that the transforming abilities of Aikido would ingrain themselves in societies around the world and the hearts of man.

CHAPTER TWENTY-ONE

The Will to Kill and Die

*"When I die, I shall soar with the angels, and when I die to
the angels, what I shall become you cannot imagine."*
—Rumi

The will to kill and to lay down one's life for a just cause are prerequisites of the Warrior path. In the chaos of combat and life-threatening self-defense situations, it is quite possible, and unfortunate, that we may be forced to take the life of an attacker or cause permanent injury. The ancient samurai concept known as Satsu Jin Kin (the sword that kills) and Katsu Jin Kin (the life-giving sword) is the source of countless classic Japanese literature written by enlightened samurai and ingrained in every Aikido technique.

Saotome Sensei teaches Kappo, or the original Daito Ryu Aiki Jiu Jitsu, or the killing art, which is the foundation of all Aikido technique, but hidden from novice students. It is simple to kill or maim an attacker permanently. The human body is frail and can be easily destroyed by a martial artist whose skill level is competent and whose spirit has been compromised by his own ego and lust for his enemy's blood. Only through strenuous training, unification of wills, and the humility of love that follows, can a Warrior gain the ability to make a split-second life-and-death decision to disarm instead of destroying or to subdue instead of kill.

Every life is sacred, and, as Warriors in pursuit of the ultimate attainment, we must practice daily and train ourselves so diligently that this choice of life or death and martial abilities become our reality, not just another YouTube video. Train yourself daily with the spirit of O'Sensei at your back. Invite him to share with you his vast wisdom and sacred vision so that you, too, may rise above the futility of war and the destruction, darkness, and pain heaped on ourselves and others by our own egoic fears and desires to win at any cost.

O'Sensei taught that the power of love was the greatest weapon of all. With love in our hearts, there is no opening for the enemy to exploit and no weakness to expose. What must we endure, how many sacrifices must we make to open our hearts and minds to this concept and to manifest it in life and death? Who could we become if our Warrior hearts overflowed with the impervious shield of love and the incredible responsibility to protect life in all its forms, and to sacrifice all for this attainment?

Think of the implications of this philosophy becoming hard-wired into our soldiers, law enforcement, and civilian sentinels. Imagine the impact this concept could have on stress, PTSD, and the addictions of our young soldiers, as they battle with the scars of war. Yes, war is hell. Yes, combat and killing are ugly, cruel, and inhumane. But, if our soldiers, law enforcement, and civilian sentinels were trained to kill only as a last resort and only if a humanitarian or self-defense situation presented itself, killing becomes life giving, not life taking.

Imagine our politicians taking on this immense responsibility and finally coming to terms with their flagrant, war-mongering ways and end the privatization and commercialization of war. Imagine America, finally standing for the words written in its Constitution. Envision Lady Liberty wielding the life-giving sword for the sake of freedom alone. Visualize America standing united behind the shield of love. A pipe dream or fairytale? We will never know what and who we can be if we continue sitting on the sidelines.

Below are a few of O'Sensei's quotations compiled from his collected talks, poems, and from oral tradition. Read these quotes with an earnest heart, stopping along the way to meditate on them. O'Sensei's words are that of an enlightened sage. His messages of peace and love are the unifying language of all humanity and the single source of inspiration for all ancient saints scattered across infinite space and time.

- "The Art of Peace begins with you. Work on yourself and your appointed task in the Art of Peace. Everyone has a spirit that can be refined, a body that can be trained in some manner, a suitable path to follow. You are here for no other purpose than to realize your inner divinity and manifest your innate enlightenment. Foster peace in your own life and then apply the Art to all that you encounter."

- "One does not need buildings, money, power, or status to practice the Art of Peace. Heaven is right where you are standing, and that is the place to train."

- "All things, material and spiritual, originate from one source and are related as if they were one family. The past, present, and future are all contained in the life force. The universe emerged and developed from one source, and we evolved through the optimal process of unification and harmonization."

- "The Art of Peace is medicine for a sick world. There is evil and disorder in the world because people have forgotten that all things emanate from one source. Return to that source and leave behind all self-centered thoughts, petty desires, and anger. Those who are possessed by nothing possess everything."

- "If you have not linked yourself to true emptiness, you will never understand the Art of Peace."

- "The Art of Peace functions everywhere on earth, in realms ranging from the vastness of space down to the tiniest plants and animals. The life force is all-pervasive and its strength boundless. The Art of Peace allows us to perceive and tap into that tremendous reserve of universal energy."

- "Life is growth. If we stop growing, technically and spiritually, we are as good as dead. The Art of Peace is a celebration of the bonding of heaven, earth, and humankind. It is all that is true, good, and beautiful."

- "Now and again, it is necessary to seclude yourself among deep mountains and hidden valleys to restore your link to the source of life. Breathe in and let yourself soar to the ends of the universe; breathe out and bring the cosmos back inside. Next, breathe up all fecundity and vibrancy of the earth. Finally, blend the breath of heaven and the breath of earth with your own, becoming the Breath of Life itself."

- "All the principles of heaven and earth are living inside you. Life itself is the truth, and this will never change. Everything in heaven and earth breathes. Breath is the thread that ties creation together. When the myriad variations in the universal breath can be sensed, the individual techniques of the Art of Peace are born."

- "Consider the ebb and flow of the tide. When waves come to strike the shore, they crest and fall, creating a sound. Your breath should follow the same pattern, absorbing the entire universe in your belly with each inhalation. Know that we all have access to four treasures: the energy of the sun and moon, the breath of heaven, the breath of earth, and the ebb and flow of the tide."

- "Those who practice the Art of Peace must protect the domain of Mother Nature, the divine reflection of creation, and keep it lovely and fresh. Warriorship gives birth to natural beauty. The subtle techniques of a Warrior arise as naturally as the appearance of spring, summer, autumn, and winter. Warriorship is none other than the vitality that sustains all life."

- "When life is victorious, there is birth; when it is thwarted, there is death. A Warrior is always engaged in a life-and-death struggle for peace."

- "Contemplate the workings of this world, listen to the words of the wise, and take all that is good as your own. With this as your base, open your own door to truth. Do not overlook the truth that is right before you. Study how water flows in a valley stream, smoothly and freely between the rocks. Also learn from holy books and wise people. Everything—even mountains, rivers, plants and trees—should be your teacher."

- "Create each day anew by clothing yourself with heaven and earth, bathing yourself with wisdom and love, and placing yourself in the heart of Mother Nature."

- "Peace originates with the flow of things—its heart is like the movement of the wind and waves. The Way is like the veins that circulate blood through our bodies, following the natural flow of the life force. If you are separated in the slightest from that divine essence, you are far off the path."

- "Your heart is full of fertile seeds, waiting to sprout. Just as a lotus flower springs from the mire to bloom splendidly, the interaction of the cosmic breath causes the flower of the spirit to bloom and bear fruit in this world."

- "Study the teachings of the pine tree, the bamboo, and the plum blossom. The pine is evergreen, firmly rooted, and venerable. The bamboo is strong, resilient, unbreakable. The plum blossom is hardy, fragrant, and elegant."

- "Always keep your mind as bright and clear as the vast sky, the great ocean, and the highest peak, empty of all thoughts. Always keep your body filled with light and heat. Fill yourself with the power of wisdom and enlightenment."

- "The penetrating brilliance of swords wielded by followers of the Way strikes at the evil enemy lurking deep within their own souls and bodies."

- "The Art of Peace is not easy. It is a fight to the finish, the slaying of evil desires and all falsehood within. On occasion the Voice of Peace resounds like thunder, jolting human beings out of their stupor."

- "To practice properly the Art of Peace, you must: Calm the spirit and return to the source. Cleanse the body and spirit by removing all malice, selfishness, and desire. Be ever grateful for the gifts received from the universe, your family, Mother Nature, and your fellow human beings."

- "The Art of Peace is based on Four Great Virtues: Bravery, Wisdom, Love, and Friendship, symbolized by Fire, Heaven, Earth, and Water."

- "The essence of the Art of Peace is to cleanse yourself of maliciousness, to get in tune with your environment, and to clear your path of all obstacles and barriers."

- "The only cure for materialism is the cleansing of the six senses (eyes, ears, nose, tongue, body, and mind). If the senses are clogged, one's perception is stifled. The more it is stifled, the more contaminated the senses become. This creates disorder in the world, and that is the greatest evil of all. Polish the heart, free the six senses and let them function without obstruction, and your entire body and soul will glow."

- "All life is a manifestation of the spirit, the manifestation of love. And the Art of Peace is the purest form of that principle. A Warrior is charged with bringing a halt to all contention and strife. Universal love functions in many forms; each manifestation should be allowed free expression. The Art of Peace is true democracy."

- "Each and every master, regardless of the era or place, heard the call and attained harmony with heaven and earth. There are many paths leading to the top of Mount Fuji, but there is only one summit—love."

- "Loyalty and devotion lead to bravery. Bravery leads to the spirit of self-sacrifice. The spirit of self-sacrifice creates trust in the power of love."

- The Art of Peace does not rely on weapons or brute force to succeed; instead, we put ourselves in tune with the universe, maintain peace in our own realms, nurture life, and prevent death and destruction. The true meaning of the term samurai is one who serves and adheres to the power of love."

- "Your mind should be in harmony with the functioning of the universe; your body should be in tune with the movement of the universe; body and mind should be bound as one, unified with the activity of the universe."

- "Daily training in the Art of Peace allows your inner divinity to shine brighter and brighter. Do not concern yourself with the right and wrong of others. Do not be calculating or act unnaturally. Keep your mind set on the Art of Peace, and do not criticize other teachers or traditions. The Art of Peace never restrains, restricts, or shackles anything. It embraces all and purifies everything."

- "Those who are enlightened never stop forging themselves. The realizations of such masters cannot be expressed well in words or by theories. The most perfect actions echo the patterns found in nature."

- "Day after day train your heart out, refining your technique: Use the one to strike the many! That is the discipline of the Warrior."

- "The purpose of training is to tighten up the slack, toughen the body, and polish the spirit."

- "Iron is full of impurities that weaken it; through forging, it becomes steel and is transformed into razor-sharp sword. Human beings develop in the same fashion."

- "The Way of a Warrior is based on humanity, love, and sincerity; the heart of martial valor is true bravery, wisdom, love, and friendship. Emphasis on the physical aspects of warriorship is futile, for the power of the body is always limited."

- "A true Warrior is always armed with three things: the radiant sword of pacification; the mirror of bravery, wisdom, and friendship; and the precious jewel of enlightenment."

CHAPTER TWENTY-TWO

Morality

"The first step in the evolution of ethics is a sense of solidarity with other human beings."
—Albert Schweitzer

As we ponder the great words of O'Sensei and reflect on his spirit, we begin to appreciate the absolute necessity of adhering to a strict moral code that honors ourselves, our Warrior ancestors, and even our enemies. Morality is a much more complex phenomena than we may realize. Our sense of justice, right, and wrong, are ideas that seem to run throughout the entire animal kingdom.

Recently, a groundbreaking study using laboratory rats proved this to be the case. The study placed two rats together, attempting to get them to play. One rat was older and substantially larger than his cousin. Rats are remarkably like dogs, kittens, or even young children when it comes to motivation levels to play with one another. Play builds many survival mechanisms in mammals, including socialization skills and techniques used in hunting and evading capture, as well as the necessary development of strong muscles, connective tissue, and bone. To begin the experiment, the scientist measured the motivation levels of the juvenile rat and its desire to play with its senior study companion.

At first, the motivation levels of the juvenile rat were measured at maximal ratings. As time went by, the scientists were able to demonstrate a substantial decline in motivation, if the senior, larger rat did not allow his juvenile companion to win during play at least thirty percent of the time. If the senior rat continued to win most of the time (greater than seventy percent), the juvenile rat would cease to play entirely.

Similar studies have been performed with other animals, including chimpanzees, that show remarkably similar results. Studies like these demonstrate that a sense of fairness is deeply embedded in the psyche of all mammals. This includes human beings. It may seem bizarre to say that the animals we often equate as pests or rodents have a sense of morality and can distinguish between right and wrong, but it seems to be true.

We have the benefit of pairing objective science with the subjective, instinctive feelings we all experience. Our sense of fairness is combined with a hard-wired, genetically shared predisposition to do no harm to our fellow man. These qualities are ingrained in all animals and are not learned behaviors; they are divine. Morality is shared principles concerning the distinction between right and wrong behaviors and is imprinted by our Maker in the DNA of all life forms.

CHAPTER TWENTY-THREE

The Code of the Warrior

"Don't ever think the reason I am peaceful is because I do not like to be violent."
—**Unknown**

As human civilizations formed into collaborative efforts and shared thoughts on morality, the need of a select group of men arose to protect this collaboration. These groups, called tribes, stood in defense against assaults from more aggressive, neighboring affiliations. As the rise of the Warrior tradition expanded across all organized societies, so did their adoption of a shared moral code.

I continue to be blown away by the divine nature in which warrior cultures throughout time and vast geographic separations came to the same shared beliefs. From ancient Greece to the Aztec nation, the warrior tradition became the embodiment of morality whose sacrifice in battle catapulted our evolutionary ascent from one of survival to one of faith. At some point in human evolution, the entirety of man shifted its consciousness and willingness to kill its own kind, not only for the sake of survival, but also for the sake of ideas and shared beliefs.

Nowhere is this truer than the rise of knighthood in ancient Europe. The development of chivalry (code of the knighthood) went hand-in-hand with the rise of knighthood, beginning around the time of the Norman conquest of England in 1066. The word *chivalry* is derived from the Medieval Latin word (caballarius), meaning horseman. In the early days, knights were largely mercenaries who offered their fighting skills and servitude to the local chieftain or warlord.

As time progressed, the knight transitioned from a hired gun to a symbol of respect and a protector of all that was good in mankind and his societies. By the eleventh and twelfth centuries, you begin to see the rise of Chivalry spread across Europe and find its way into popular literature. From its origin, knighthood became almost synonymous with Christianity. As this devotion and a call to arms by the Catholic popes spread throughout Europe, the rise of the Knights Templar and the four Christian Crusades were born.

In the Middles Ages, the Crusades were an almost continuous series of military-religious campaigns, inspired by the pagan papacy and led by European Christians and their kings, with the goal of securing the Holy Land from the infidel Turks. From 1096 until nearly 1300, the Crusaders, traveling in great armies or as individual pilgrims, journeyed to the Holy Land to wage war against Muslims who had conquered Jerusalem in 638 AD. Muslims had become a serious perceived threat to Christianity, and especially the Roman Catholic Church, after Muslim raiding parties brutally attacked unprotected Christian pilgrims throughout the Holy Land.

Although some of the Knights Templar fought for glory and riches, religious faith inspired thousands upon thousands of these soldiers of the Cross. When the Crusades began,

Europeans still lived in the so-called Dark Ages. Before the campaigns ended, the West stood on the threshold of the modern era and the dominance of the Roman Catholic Church. This worldwide dominance was built on the backs of the faithful and by the manipulation of otherwise honorable men.

From 1096 until the death of the last Conquistador Juan De Onate in 1626, the papacy engaged in a feverous, genocidal conquest of the globe, decimating the indigenous populations of North and South America and sowing the seeds of distrust and hatred amongst Muslims and Christians that is still being played out today.

The Knights Templar rose to great power and prominence. They were later ostracized and demonized as heretics by the very papacy that inspired their two-hundred years long campaign to secure the holy lands and the birthplace of Jesus of Nazareth —all in the name of God.

In hindsight, we cannot deny the brutality and darkness surrounding these conquests. Although the Templars' efforts were misguided, we cannot dispense or rewrite history when it conveniently suits us. It is not my goal to glamorize the Knights Templar or to justify the killing of another for beliefs of any kind. My goal in discussing the Templars is to forgive them of their barbarism so we can see truth in their efforts and lay blame where it truly belongs — at the feet of the wicked papacy of the Medieval era.

The Templars were the culmination of centuries of Warrior knights who swore a blood oath to protect God, king, and country. Their love and passion to serve God was inexcusably weaponized to promote the power and conquest of the Roman Catholic Church and, more specifically, the papacy. As

Warriors for God, we should never forget this atrocity, for those who forget their history are doomed to repeat it.

The Templar Moral Code

Love that which is good; ignore that which is bad!
Be goodness, justice, and compassion; never criticize!
Be pure, compassionate, and gentle; never use irony!
Be patient, calm and considerate; never give in to
anger or pride!
Be confident, satisfied, and open to others; do not doubt
and be not envious!
Be moderate in all things; avoid excesses!
Be humble, kind, modest, generous, and respectful of
others; never be spiteful!
Be true in words and deeds, tell the truth; never lie and
never slander!
Be helpful and considerate of all there is; never deceive
nor betray anyone!
Love and protect Life, spread Peace and Harmony; in no
way, be aggressive!

CHAPTER TWENTY-FOUR

The Modern Warrior

"There are but three beings worthy of respect: the priest,
the warrior, and the poet. To know, to kill, and to create.
The rest of mankind may be taxed and drudged,
they are born for the stable, that is to say,
to practice what they call professions."
—Charles Baudelaire

As society progresses from the conquests of the Dark Ages to the rise of artificial intelligence, fake news, and political malevolence, morality is more important today than ever before. Our modern society and its leaders drive a wedge between its peoples, promoting hatred, bigotry, and intolerance. They do this to create identity politics and infuse a tribal mentality in THEIR constituency in a throwback to the Stone Age.

It is preposterous to conceptualize that, at our most advanced stage of development in human history, we find ourselves reverting to the tribal, barbaric behaviors of our chimpanzee cousins. As men who decide to unsheathe the sword of the Warrior tradition, we must also take up the code of our warrior ancestors and their universal sense of morality.

Never forget the core of the Warrior heart, which is the unified will, oriented by love and our moral compass, alongside our willingness to kill or die for the sake of our faith, *not* our beliefs. The values we hold dear have been handed down by our ancestors for thousands of years. The innate truths they represent form the basis of our spiritual paths. It is more important than ever, given the dilemma we find ourselves in, to forgo the promises and delusions of modern society, today's Church and state, and replace them with the wisdom of the ages and the eternal lessons of the Holy Bible.

For example, in the Old Testament, the struggles of Moses and the gift of the Ten Commandments by God Himself is one of the most celebrated stories in biblical history. In 1446 BC, God gave Moses a set of commandments by which the Israelites were to live. These Commandments, written in stone, are:

1. You shall have no other gods before Me.

2. You shall make no idols.

3. You shall not take the name of the Lord your God in vain.

4. Keep the Sabbath day holy.

5. Honor your father and your mother.

6. You shall not murder.

7. You shall not commit adultery.

8. You shall not steal.

9. You shall not bear false witness against your neighbor.

10. You shall not covet.

When we pair the timeless truths of the Ten Commandments with the teachings given to us by Jesus of Nazareth, we form a complete picture of morality. We have been handed down a complete glossary of texts to reference, so that we, as men, always conduct ourselves accordingly and honor our Warrior tradition. I am quoting these texts from the King James Version of the Bible because I appreciate the power and beauty of its soul-stirring language:

- **Repent**

"From that time Jesus began to preach, and to say, Repent: for the kingdom of heaven is at hand" (Matthew 4:17).

- **Follow Me**

"And he saith unto them, follow me, and I will make you fishers of men" (Matthew 4:19).

- **Rejoice**

"Blessed are ye, when men shall revile you, and persecute you, and shall say all manner of evil against you falsely, for my sake. Rejoice, and be exceeding glad: for great is your reward in heaven: for so persecuted they the prophets which were before you" (Matthew 5:11–12).

- **Let Your Light Shine**

"Let your light so shine before men, that they may see your good works, and glorify your Father which is in heaven" (Matthew 5:16).

- **Honor God's Law**

"Think not that I am come to destroy the law, or the prophets: I am not come to destroy, but to fulfill" (Matthew 5:17).

- **Be Reconciled**

"Therefore, if thou bring thy gift to the altar, and there rememberest that thy brother hath aught against thee; leave there thy gift before the altar and go thy way; first be reconciled to thy brother, and then come and offer thy gift" (Matthew 5:23–25).

- **Do Not Lust**

"But I say unto you, that whosoever looketh on a woman to lust after her hath committed adultery with her already in his heart. And if thy right eye offend thee, pluck it out, and cast it from thee: for it is profitable for thee that one of thy members should perish, and not that thy whole body should be cast into hell. And if thy right hand offends thee, cut it off, and cast it from thee: for it is profitable for thee that one of thy members should perish, and not that thy whole body should be cast into hell" (Matthew 5:28–30).

- **Keep Your Word**

"Let your communication be, Yea, yea; Nay, nay: for what-soever is more than these cometh of evil" (Matthew 5:37).

- **Go the Second Mile**

"Ye have heard that it hath been said, An eye for an eye, and a tooth for a tooth: but I say unto you, That ye resist not evil: but whosoever shall smite thee on thy right cheek, turn to him the other also. And if any man will sue thee at the law, and take away thy coat, let him have thy cloak also. And whosoever shall compel thee to go a mile, go with him twain. Give to him that asketh thee, and from him that would borrow of thee turn not thou away" (Matthew 5:38–42).

- **Love Your Enemies**

"But I say unto you, Love your enemies, bless them that curse you, do good to them that hate you, and pray for them which despitefully use you, and persecute you; that ye may be the children of your Father which is in heaven: for he maketh his sun to rise on the evil and on the good, and sendeth rain on the just and on the unjust. For if ye love them which love you, what reward have ye? Do not even the publicans the same?" (Matthew 5:44–46).

- **Be Perfect**

"If ye love them which love you, what reward have ye? do not even the publicans the same? And if ye salute your brethren

only, what do ye more than others? do not even the publicans so? Be ye therefore perfect, even as your Father which is in heaven is perfect" (Matthew 5:46–48).

• **Practice Secret Disciplines**

". . .When thou doest thine alms, let not thy left hand know what thy right hand doeth: that thine alms may be in secret: and thy Father which seeth in secret himself shall reward thee openly... When thou prayest, enter into thy closet, and when thou hast shut thy door, pray to thy Father which is in secret; and thy Father which seeth in secret shall reward thee openly... When thou fastest, anoint thine head, and wash thy face; that thou appear not unto men to fast, but unto thy Father which is in secret: and thy Father, which seeth in secret, shall reward thee openly" (Matthew 6:1–18).

• **Lay Up Treasures**

"Lay not up for yourselves treasures upon earth, where moth and rust doth corrupt, and where thieves break through and steal: but lay up for yourselves treasures in heaven, where neither moth nor rust doth corrupt, and where thieves do not break through nor steal: for where your treasure is, there will your heart be also" (Matthew 6:19–21).

• **Seek God's Kingdom**

"Seek ye first the kingdom of God, and his righteousness; and all these things shall be added unto you" (Matthew 6:33).

- **Judge Not**

"Judge not, that ye be not judged. For with what judgment ye judge, ye shall be judged: and with what measure ye mete, it shall be measured to you again. And why beholdest thou the mote that is in thy brother's eye, but considerest not the beam that is in thine own eye?" (Matthew 7:1–3).

- **Do Not Cast Pearls**

"Give not that which is holy unto the dogs, neither cast ye your pearls before swine, lest they trample them under their feet, and turn again and rend you" (Matthew 7:6).

- **Ask, Seek, Knock**

"Ask, and it shall be given you; seek, and ye shall find; knock, and it shall be opened unto you: for everyone that asketh receiveth; and he that seeketh findeth; and to him that knocketh it shall be opened" (Matthew 7:7–8).

- **Do unto Others**

"Therefore, all things whatsoever ye would that men should do to you, do ye even so to them: for this is the law and the prophets" (Matthew 7:12).

- **Choose the Narrow Way**

"Enter ye in at the strait gate: for wide is the gate, and broad is the way, that leadeth to destruction, and many there

be which go in there at: because strait is the gate, and narrow is the way, which leadeth unto life, and few there be that find it" (Matthew 7:13–14).

- **Beware of False Prophets**

"Beware of false prophets, which come to you in sheep's clothing, but inwardly they are ravening wolves. Ye shall know them by their fruits. Do men gather grapes of thorns, or figs of thistles?" (Matthew 7:15–16).

- **Pray for Laborers**

"The harvest truly is plenteous, but the laborers are few; pray ye therefore the Lord of the harvest, that he will send forth laborers into his harvest" (Matthew 9:37–38).

- **Be Wise as Serpents**

"Behold, I send you forth as sheep in the midst of wolves be ye therefore wise as serpents, and harmless as doves" (Matthew 10:16).

- **Fear Not**

"Fear not them which kill the body but are not able to kill the soul: but rather fear him which is able to destroy both soul and body in hell" (Matthew 10:28).

- **Hear God's Voice**

"He that hath ears to hear, let him hear" (Matthew 11:15).

- **Take My Yoke**

"Come unto me, all ye that labor and are heavy laden, and I will give you rest. Take my yoke upon you and learn of me; for I am meek and lowly in heart: and ye shall find rest unto your souls. For my yoke is easy, and my burden is light" (Matthew 11:28–30).

- **Honor Your Parents**

"For God commanded, saying, honor thy father and mother: and, he that curseth father or mother, let him die the death" (Matthew 15:4).

- **Beware of Leaven**

"Take heed and beware of the leaven of the Pharisees and of the Sadducees" (Matthew 16:6).

- **Deny Yourself**

"If any man will come after me, let him deny himself, and take up his cross daily, and follow me. For whosoever will save his life shall lose it: but whosoever will lose his life for my sake, the same shall save it. For what is a man advantaged, if he gains the whole world, and lose himself, or be cast away?" (Luke 9:23–25).

• Despise Not Little Ones

"Take heed that ye despise not one of these little ones; for I say unto you, that in heaven their angels do always behold the face of my Father which is in heaven" (Matthew 18:10).

• Go to Offenders

"Moreover, if thy brother shall trespass against thee, go and tell him his fault between thee and him alone: if he shall hear thee, thou hast gained thy brother. But if he will not hear thee, then take with thee one or two more, that in the mouth of two or three witnesses every word may be established. And if he neglects to hear them, tell it unto the church: but if he neglects to hear the church, let him be unto thee as a heathen man and a publican" (Matthew 18:15–17).

• Beware of Covetousness

"And he said unto them, take heed, and beware of covetousness: for a man's life consisteth not in the abundance of the things which he possesseth" (Luke 12:15).

• Forgive Offenders

"Then came Peter to him, and said, Lord, how oft shall my brother sin against me, and I forgive him? till seven times? Jesus saith unto him, I say not unto thee, Until seven times: but, Until seventy times seven" (Matthew 18:21–22).

- **Honor Marriage**

"And he answered and said unto them, have ye not read, that he which made them at the beginning made them male and female, and said, for this cause shall a man leave father and mother, and shall cleave to his wife: and they twain shall be one flesh? Wherefore they are no more twain, but one flesh. What therefore God hath joined together, let not man put asunder" (Matthew 19:4–6).

- **Be a Servant**

". . .Whosoever will be great among you, let him be your minister; and whosoever will be chief among you, let him be your servant: even as the Son of man came not to be ministered unto, but to minister, and to give his life a ransom for many" (Matthew 20:26–28).

- **Be a House of Prayer**

"It is written, my house shall be called the house of prayer..." (Matthew 21:13).

- **Ask in Faith**

"Verily I say unto you, if ye have faith, and doubt not, ye shall not only do this which is done to the fig tree, but also if ye shall say unto this mountain, be thou removed, and be thou cast into the sea: it shall be done. And all things, whatsoever ye shall ask in prayer, believing, ye shall receive" (Matthew 21:21–22).

- **Bring in the Poor**

"Then said he also to him that bade him, when thou makest a dinner or a supper, call not thy friends, nor thy brethren, neither thy kinsmen, nor thy rich neighbors; lest they also bid thee again, and a recompense have made thee. But when thou makest a feast, call the poor, the maimed, the lame, the blind: and thou shalt be blessed; for they cannot recompense thee: for thou shalt be recompensed at the resurrection of the just" (Luke 14:12–14).

- **Render to Caesar**

"Show me the tribute money. And they brought unto him a penny. And he saith unto them, whose is this image and superscription? They say unto him, Caesar's. Then saith he unto them, render therefore unto Caesar the things which are Caesar's; and unto God the things that are God's" (Matthew 22:19–21).

- **Love the Lord**

"Jesus said unto him, thou shalt love the Lord thy God with all thy heart, and with all thy soul, and with all thy mind. This is the first and great commandment" (Matthew 22:37–38).

- **Love Your Neighbor**

"And the second [commandment] is like unto it, thou shalt love thy neighbor as thyself. On these two commandments hang all the law and the prophets" (Matthew 22:39–40).

- **Await My Return**

"Watch therefore: for ye know not what hour your Lord doth come. But know this, that if the goodman of the house had known in what watch the thief would come, he would have watched, and would not have suffered his house to be broken up. Therefore, be ye also ready: for in such an hour as ye think not the Son of man cometh" (Matthew 24:42–44).

- **Take, Eat, and Drink**

"As they were eating, Jesus took bread, and blessed it, and broke it, and gave it to the disciples, and said, Take, eat; this is my body. And he took the cup, and gave thanks, and gave it to them, saying, Drink ye all of it; for this is my blood of the New Testament, which is shed for many for the remission of sins" (Matthew 26:26–28).

- **Be Born Again**

"Jesus answered, Verily, verily, I say unto thee, except a man be born of water and of the Spirit, he cannot enter into the kingdom of God. That which is born of the flesh is flesh; and that which is born of the Spirit is spirit. Marvel not that I said unto thee, Ye must be born again" (John 3:5–7).

- **Keep My Commandments**

"If ye love me, keep my commandments" (John 14:15).

- **Watch and Pray**

"Watch and pray, that ye enter not into temptation: the spirit indeed is willing, but the flesh is weak" (Matthew 26:41).

- **Feed My Sheep**

"So, when they had dined, Jesus saith to Simon Peter, Simon, son of John, lovest thou me more than these? He saith unto him, Yea, Lord; thou knowest that I love thee. He saith unto him, Feed my lambs. He saith to him again the second time, Simon, son of John, lovest thou me? He saith unto him, Yea, Lord; thou knowest that I love thee. He saith unto him, Feed my sheep" (John 21:15–16).

- **Baptize My Disciples**

"Go ye therefore, and teach all nations, baptizing them in the name of the Father, and of the Son, and of the Holy Ghost" (Matthew 28:19).

- **Receive God's Power**

"And behold, I send the promise of my Father upon you: but tarry ye in the city of Jerusalem, until ye be endued with power from on high" (Luke 24:49).

- **Make Disciples**

"Go ye therefore and teach all nations... teaching them to observe all things whatsoever I have commanded you: and, lo,

I am with you always, even unto the end of the world. Amen"
(Matthew 28:19–20).

Take Up Your Cross

Never forget it is your duty to protect and love all sentient
creatures and to remain vigilant. Reward yourself for walking
the razor's edge with the greatest gift a man can give himself:
honor. We have at our disposal the great works compiled in the
Holy Bible, the ancient saints, and the teachings left to us by
the greatest warriors who ever lived.

Take up your cross as Jesus asks of you. See the universal
truths arising in nature and in your own being, as defined in the
immortal words of O'Sensei. Pay homage to the sacrifice and
courage of the Knights Templar, as they lay down their lives
for their brothers at arms and shed their blood for their beloved
Christ. Let us learn from the mistakes of those who have come
before, as we wrestle with the harsh realities of self-defense
and warfare.

Let us be humble, silence our minds, and turn our ears
toward our hearts. Pray constantly that our Father grants us discernment, so that the voice of our ancestors and the Holy Spirit
overpower our inner demons and egoic desires.

Turn off the noise of your mind, squash its perpetual spinning thoughts, and its addiction to the fear of tomorrow and
the regret of yesterday. Learn to be right here, right now, living
inside your immense heart that grows each day, as you give
yourself freely and consciously to suffering and the surrender
of your will to our beloved Father.

CHAPTER TWENTY-FIVE

Final Thoughts on Undaunted Courage

"Hardships often prepare ordinary people
for an extraordinary destiny."
—C.S. Lewis

One of my all-time favorite books, *Undaunted Courage* by Steven Ambrose, details the incredible saga of the 1803 expedition of Captain Meriwether Lewis and Captain William Clark, who led a voyage up the Missouri River to the Rockies, over the mountains, down the Columbia River to the Pacific Ocean, and back. Hand-chosen by Thomas Jefferson, Lewis and Clark made the first map of the trans-Mississippi West, provided invaluable scientific data on the flora and fauna of the Louisiana Purchase territory, and established the American claim to Oregon, Washington, and Idaho.

I have spent many hours contemplating the magnitude and audacity of Jefferson's request for thirty-three capable young men to venture into the unknown, hostile wilderness of the great American West, risking life and limb for little more than the experience of having done such an impossible task. I am even more flabbergasted that not one of them refused Jefferson's challenge.

For more than three years, these hardened men canoed, hiked, dragged, lifted, and hauled twelve tons of gear over 7,690 miles. They did this while under constant threat of attack from Native Americans and across the most inhospitable environment imaginable. Just to give you some depth of understanding as to how gargantuan this task was, following is a packing list written by Lewis's own hand (misspellings and all).

Lewis & Clark Expedition Packing List[20]
Mathematical Instruments
    1 Hadley's Quadrant
    1 Mariner's Compas & 2 pole chain
    1 Set of plotting instruments
    3 Thermometers
    1 Cheap portable Microscope
    1 Pocket Compass
    1 brass Scale one foot in length
    6 Magnetic needles in small straight silver or brass cases opening on the side with hinges.
    1 Instrument for measuring made of tape with feet & inches mark'd on it

---

[20] https://www.monticello.org/thomas-jefferson/louisiana-lewis-clark/preparing-for-the-expedition/lewis-s-packing-list/

2 Hydrometers
1 Theodolite
1 Sett of planespheres
2 Artificial Horizons
1 Patent log
6 papers of Ink powder
4 Metal Pens brass or silver
1 Set of Small Slates & pencils
2 Crayons
Sealing wax one bundle
1 Miller's edition of Lineus in 2 Vol:
Books
Maps
Charts
Blank Vocabularies
Writing paper
1 Pair large brass money scales with two sets of weights.

Arms & Accoutrements

15 Rifle
15 Powder Horns & pouches complete
15 Pairs of Bullet Molds
15 do. (ditto) Of Wipers or Gun worms
15 Ball Screws
24 Pipe Tomahawks
24 large knives
Extra parts of Locks & tools for repairing arms
15 Gun Slings
500 best Flints

Ammunition

> 200 Lbs. Best rifle powder
> 400 lbs. Lead

Clothing

> 15 3 pt. Blankets
> 15 Watch Coats with Hoods & belts
> 15 Woolen Overalls
> 15 Rifle Frocks of waterproof Cloth if possible
> 30 Pairs of Socks or half Stockings
> 20 Fatigue Frocks or hinting shirts
> 30 Shirts of Strong linen
> 30 yds. Common flannel.

Camp Equipage

> 6 Copper kettles (1 of 5 Gallons, 1 of 3, 2 of 2, & 2 of 1)
> 35 falling Axes.
> 4 Drawing Knives, short & strong
> 2 Augers of the patent kind.
> 1 Small permanent Vice
> 1 Hand Vice
> 36 Gimblets assorted
> 24 Files do. (ditto)
> 12 Chisels do. (ditto)
> 10 Nails do. (ditto)
> 2 Steel plate hand saws
> 2 Vials of Phosforus
> 1 do. (ditto) Of Phosforus made of allum & sugar

4 Groce fishing Hooks assorted

12 Bunches of Drum Line

2 Foot Adzes

12 Bunches of Small cord

2 Pick Axes

3 Coils of rope

2 Spades

12 Bunches Small fishing line assorted

1 lb. Turkey or Oil Stone

1 Iron Mill for Grinding Corn

20 yds. Oil linnen for wrapping & securing Articles

10 yds do. do. (ditto) Of thicker quality for covering and lining boxes. &c

40 yds Do. Do. (ditto) To form two half faced Tents or Shelters.

4 Tin blowing Trumpets

2 hand or spiral spring Steelyards

20 yds Strong Oznaburgs (strong cloth)

24 Iron Spoons

24 Pint Tin Cups (without handles)

30 Steels for striking or making fire

100 Flints for do. do. do. (ditto)

2 Frows

6 Saddlers large Needles

6 Do. (ditto) Large Awls

Muscatoe Curtains

2 patent chamber lamps & wicks

15 Oil Cloth Bags for securing provision

1 Sea Grass Hammock

Provisions and Means of Subsistence

150 lbs. Portable Soup.
3 bushels of Allum or Rock Salt
Spicies assorted
6 Kegs of 5 Gallons each making 30 Gallons of rectified spirits such as is used for the Indian trade
6 Kegs bound with iron Hoops

Indian Presents

5 lbs. White Wampum
4 lbs. White Glass Beads mostly small
20 lbs. Red Do. Do. (ditto) Assorted
5 lbs. Yellow or Orange Do. Do. (ditto) Assorted
30 Calico Shirts
12 Pieces of East India muslin Hanckerchiefs striped or check'd with brilliant Colours.
12 Red Silk Hanckerchiefs
144 Small cheap looking Glasses
100 Burning Glasses
4 Vials of Phosforus
288 Steels for striking fire
144 Small cheap Scizors
20 Pair large Do. (ditto)
12 Groces Needles Assorted No. 1 to 8 Common points
12 Groces Do. (ditto) Assorted with points for sewing leather
288 Common brass thimbles – part W. office
10 lbs. Sewing Thread assorted
24 Hanks Sewing Silk
8 lbs. Red Lead

2 lbs. Vermillion – at War Office

288 Knives Small such as are generally used for the Indian trade, with fix'd blades & handles inlaid with brass

36 Large knives

36 Pipe Tomahawks – at H. Ferry

12 lbs. Brass wire Assorted

12 lbs. Iron do. Do. (ditto) generally large

6 Belts of narrow Ribbons colours assorted

50 lbs. Spun Tobacco.

20 Small falling axes to be obtained in Tennessee

40 fish Griggs such as the Indians use with a single barbed point – at Harper's ferry

3 Groce fishing Hooks assorted

3 Groce Mockerson awls assorted

50 lbs. Powder secured in a Keg covered with oil Cloth

24 Belts of Worsted feiret (woven wool tape) or Gartering Colours brilliant and Assorted

15 Sheets of Copper Cut into strips of an inch in width & a foot long

20 Sheets of Tin

12 lbs. Strips of Sheet iron 1 In. wide 1 foot long

1 Pc. Red Cloth second quality

1 Nest of 8 or 9 small copper kettles

100 Block-tin rings cheap kind ornamented with Colour'd Glass or Mock-Stone

2 Groces of brass Curtain Rings & sufficently large for the Finger

1 Groce Cast Iron Combs

18 Cheap brass Combs

24 Blankets.

12 Arm Bands Silver at War Office

12 Wrist do. do. Do. (ditto)
36 Ear Trinkets Do. Part do. (ditto)
6 Groces Drops of Do. Part Do. (ditto)
4 doz Rings for Fingers of do. (ditto)
4 Groces Broaches of do. (ditto)
12 Small Medals do. (ditto)

Means of Transportation

1 Keeled Boat light strong at least 60 feet in length her bur-
then equal to 8 Tons
1 Iron frame of Canoe 40 feet long
1 Large Wooden Canoe
12 Spikes for Setting-Poles
4 Boat Hooks & points Complete
2 Chains & Pad-Locks for confining the Boat & Canoes &c.

Medicine

15 lbs. Best powder's Bark
10 lbs. Epsom or Glauber Salts
4 oz. Calomel
12 oz. Opium
_ oz. Tarter emetic
8 oz. Borax
4 oz. Powder'd Ipecacuana
8 oz. Powder Jalap
8 oz. Powdered Rhubarb
6 Best lancets
2 oz. White Vitriol
4 oz. Lacteaum Saturni

4 Pewter Penis syringes

1 Flour of Sulphur

3 Clyster pipes

4 oz. Turlingtons Balsam

2 lbs. Yellow Bascilicum

2 Sticks of Symple Diachylon

1 lb. Blistering Ointments

2 lbs. Nitre

2 lbs. Coperas

One of my most beloved places on Earth is the Front Range Mountains located around Boulder, Colorado. Atop this vantage point, you can see hundreds of miles to the east across the golden, waving fields of the Great Plains. Behind you to the west, you can see the jagged, snow-capped mountains of the Continental Divide and the beginning of the seemingly insurmountable Rocky Mountain range. I have yet to make it to Lewis and Clark's famous portage site located about 700 miles to the north, over the Great Falls of the Bitter Root Mountain Range in Montana, but it is on my bucket list.

When you stand on any summit along the precipice of the Rocky Mountain Range, which stretches north and south, it's impossible to fathom how intimidating crossing this impenetrable wall must have seemed to thirty guys, carrying tons of gear.

Picture how breathtaking it must have been to experience this untamed landscape before its native peoples were driven from it—one of several, sinful mistakes made by our great nation and peoples. Nostalgia fills my soul to imagine the sight of a solo Native American warrior riding bareback across the plains, feathers blowing in his hair, bow and spear at his side, on a horse whose ancestors belonged to Spanish conquistadors more than three hundred years earlier. How incredible to sleep under the star-filled sky and awaken to the sun rising over the daunting sight of the Rocky Mountains to begin another brutal day. I would give almost anything to have been one of those thirty-three men.

I am awaked from this recurring daydream by a great sense of remorse, and foreboding thoughts invade my feeling of impending doom. I begin to wonder, does today's modern man possess the hardness, internal fortitude, hunger, and drive of our Founding Fathers and the thirty-three men of the Lewis and Clark expedition, or are those qualities now extinct? Do we as modern men have within us the wherewithal to sustain the fires of passion and level of sacrifice exhibited by Jesus Christ so that we may follow Him wherever He may lead?

Can we learn to forgo our hatred, fear, and resentment of those who have done us harm and, instead, harness the weaponry of non-violent love as taught by O'Sensei, Gandhi, and Martin Luther King? Do we still have the heart of our Templar brothers who were so willing to lay down their lives for their faith? Will any of us ever be bold enough to shine through the shadow cast by the ancient saints and walk the razor's edge as they did, or are our best days behind us? Are there any among us willing to stare death, our ultimate foe, squarely in the face, and defeat this dragon once and for all, as demonstrated by the ancient samurai and today's flow-addicted daredevils? These are questions we should ask ourselves, and the answers should keep us pacing the floors at night.

As men, we have within us the infinite, untapped potential of the cosmos. We are the children of our Lord and Savior Jesus Christ who is King of kings and Lord over Heaven and Earth (Mathew 28; 18-20). Are you willing to take up your sword and shield and join in the greatest adventure of your life, or will you sit on the sidelines? Will you lay your life down to protect your neighbor and all God's creatures, or abstain from action? Will you rise above your selfish ego, your five senses, and the addiction to earthly things, or live out your days as a slave to darkness? Will you vow to live your life by the code of the Warrior and honor your ancestors with the blood, sweat, and tears of endless pursuit, or succumb to the continual beratement of your tattered mind and broken body?

Darkness and evil are upon us, brothers. Make no mistake about it. The greatest battle of all time is here, as predicted in the book of Daniel, Ezekial and Revelation. Only the truest of us are willing and capable of donning the armor of God, even fewer may serve. Your journey begins now, this very moment, and the attacks from Lucifer himself will most certainly follow.

I leave you now, with great anticipation and a full heart, alongside the most divine words possibly ever articulated into written language. Read it for the first time through the reborn vision of the ancient saints, of which you are now a part. Let it guide and protect you on the tumultuous path that leads to union with our Heavenly Father. May it comfort you in times of strife and be a beacon of light leading you to the Kingdom of God on Earth and in Heaven.

Godspeed, my brothers. May we live out our days as free men, never veering from the razor's edge and the pursuit of the Total Warrior.

Psalm 23

The LORD is my shepherd; I shall not want.
He maketh me to lie down in green pastures: he leadeth me
beside the still waters.
He restoreth my soul: he leadeth me in the paths of righteous-
ness for his name's sake.
Yea, though I walk through the valley of the shadow of death,
I will fear no evil: for thou art with me; thy rod and thy staff
they comfort me.
Thou preparest a table before me in the presence of mine ene-
mies: thou anointest my head with oil; my cup runneth over.
Surely goodness and mercy shall follow me all the days of my
life: and I will dwell in the house of the LORD forever.
Amen

QUESTIONS FOR REFLECTION

1. *We have talked a great deal about darkness in this book. Can you see how darkness manifests in your life? Make a list of everything in your heart that may be harmful to your growth as a Man (mentally, physically, spiritually, and emotionally). Can you identify the origin of that darkness?*

2. *Can you see how Darkness has infested our government's institutions, political parties, the church and corporations? How can you become more active in your local community, city, and state to affect positive change?*

3. *In Chapter Six we discussed the importance of forgiving others. Can you forgive those who have done you harm? Write a small letter to every person who has harmed you and forgive them for their trespasses. Can you see how harboring resentment toward them has harmed you? Describe?*

4. *Do you realize the impact of social media and our addiction to smart phones has on our lives? How has it impacted your life and those of your family and loved ones? How can you end your reliance on these technologies?*

5. *Describe your current relationship with God? Do you desire a closer more intimate relationship? Explain.*

6. *In our discussion on "The Way of the Warrior," we talked about the concept of "the false self." How Does*

the False Self manifest in your life? What are the differences between your "true self" and the "false self"? How can you begin to let go of the addictions of the false self?

7. *Do you recognize the Warrior in you? Do you celebrate him or push him down? How can tapping into your inner Warrior benefit your life? Please explain in detail.*

8. *Rank in order your greatest fears (Death, illness, poverty, old age). Sit in silence with perfect posture. As you breathe in ask yourself "can I let go of my fear of (state your list in chronological order for each of the four topics)?*

   As you breathe out answer it with a yes or no. Then, will I let go of my fear of_____. Finally, breath in as you ask yourself the final question, When? As you exhale say to yourself "Now". Describe the experience of this exercise?

9. *Describe in your own words the concept of Mu Ju No Shin, (No abiding mind). How can this mindset aid you in life?*

10. *Have you ever experienced Flow? Where? When? How can learning to induce the Flow State at will harm or help you in life?*

11. *List the attributes of your left and right brains. Which is dominant? How does the imbalance effect your life? How could balancing the left and right brains effect your life?*

244

12. *What does it mean to you to "Follow Me"? (Chapter 24) How has the Church either aided or inhibited your spiritual growth? How can you grow Mentally, emotionally, physically, and spiritually to become closer to God?*

13. *Describe in your own words the Trinity concept? How does it manifest in your experience? Do you know the True Gospel and the Five Solas? Research the Reformation of the Church and the reasons for that Reformation. Deepen yourself in the true Gospel, never letting a moment pass where its power and promise are not first and foremost in your Heart and Mind.*

14. *What are your addictions to the Flesh? Earthly possessions? How can releasing them aid in your spiritual growth?*

15. *How can consciously accepting your suffering aid you in your spiritual life? Can you see how your suffering is unique to you? Why did God choose these vehicles of suffering just for you? What does he want you to learn? Pray and ask for his wisdom and write what he says:*

16. *How can embracing the Suck increase your individual will and character? How does increasing your will benefit God when combined with his?*

17. *What are you most passionate about? How can you use your passion to help humanity?*

18. *What would you die for? What would you be willing to kill for? How can self-defense be acceptable in the eyes of God?*

19. *How does morality and living your life by the Code of the Warrior impact your life and the lives of your family and loved ones?*

20. *Film yourself doing five bodyweight squats. Notice how you stand? Are you able to squat below parallel and stand back up with spinal integrity? How can you begin to make incremental changes to your effect healthy posture? Why is it important?*

21. *Are you currently exercising? If not, how can you begin? Create a doable plan and schedule appropriately. If so, how can you work on weakness and areas of concern? What are your likes and dislikes? List them. Focus on your dislikes and fit them into your current fitness program.*

22. *How is physical health associated with mental, emotional and spiritual health? What are the addictions of the five senses or Earthly possessions which interfere with your pursuit of physical health?*

23. *How can the study of self-defense and martial arts benefit you? What are the obstacles to begin training? How can you overcome those obstacles and what would that act imply?*

24. *How can you better prepare for an emergency situation both short and long term? Make a list of all basic essentials (food, water, shelter, self-defense, transportation, energy or fuel, communication, etc.) Grade yourself A-F in each category and make a plan for how to remedy each situation.*

25. *What does the Constitution of the United States mean to you? How important is your personal freedom and a free Republic? How can you take part in becoming an activist for Freedom of all peoples? What would happen to the world if the United States were to fail as a free Republic?*

26. *What has this book taught you? How will it affect your life? What do you need to change to become all God intended you to be? How are you going to get there? How much does it mean to reach your full potential?*

27. *How can you help a friend, family or loved one realize their own personal Christ Consciousness and why is it important?*

About the Author

Stewart Breeding is a master trainer, performance coach, martial artist and former National Champion Power-lifter. He is a combat veteran of the 82nd Airborne and a devout Christian greatly influenced by the works of St. John of the Cross, St. Francis of Assisi, Thomas Merton, Alan Watts, D.T. Suzuki, Father Thomas Keating, James Finley, and master theologians Dr. Chuck Missler, Dr. John MacArthur, Dr. Michael Brown, R.C. Sproul, Dr. James White, and Pastor Jeff Durbin from Apologia Church.

Stewart has worked extensively with Zen Master Dennis Merzel (Genpo Roshi) and Yogi Jaggi Vasudev (Sadhguru,) founder of Isha Yoga. He is the author of three books—*Limitless* (2010), *Biohacker* (2017), and *The Total Warrior* (2022). Stewart is available for public speaking engagements. Stewart can be contacted through www.stewartbreeding.com *or www.thetotalwa*rrior.com. Please follow Stewart on Instagram and also The Total Warrior Youtube page.

CPSIA information can be obtained
at www.ICGtesting.com
Printed in the USA
BVHW041516170622
640070BV00011B/115/J